Cosmic Grandma
Wisdom

Also by Lauren O. Thyme

The Lemurian Way: Remembering your Essential Nature
(also translated into Turkish and published
in Turkey by Akasa Publishers)
Along the Nile
Strangers in Paradise
Twin Souls: A Karmic Love Story
Forgiveness Equals Fortune, co-authored with Liah Holtzman
Thymely Tales: Transformational Fairy Tales for Adults and Children
From the Depths of Thyme: Poems of Life, Sex, and Transformation
Alternatives for Everyone
Coming soon: *Catherine, a true story*

Cosmic Grandma Wisdom

Lauren O. Thyme

Lauren O. Thyme Publishing

Sante Fe

2017

A compilation of articles first appearing in
fatemag.com and *galdepress.com* © Lauren O. Thyme.
"Battle of Beliefs" Lauren O. Thyme © 2011 *collapsenet.com*
"Contemplating Survival" Lauren O. Thyme © 2009 *collapsenet.com*
"Removing Fear From My Heart" Lauren O. Thyme © 2010 *collapsenet.com*
"Gratitude" Excerpted from *The Lemurian Way*
by Lauren O. Thyme with Sareya Orion, ©2000
"My Life With Faeries and Devas" Lauren O. Thyme © 2011 *Fate* Sept/Oct 2011

ISBN 978-0-9983446-2-1

Cover Image by Ambur Rockell West, artist, singer,
songwriter, author, and granddaughter of Lauren O. Thyme
Facebook: Ambur Rockell West
Email: lilmissbur@gmail.com
https://www.etsy.com/people/Amburtcb
youtube.com ambur rockell

Interior and Cover Design by Sue Stein

Contact Lauren O. Thyme:
Email: thyme.lauren@gmail.com
Facebook: Lauren O. Thyme
LaurenOThymeCreations.com

*Dedicated with love and kisses
to my children, Andrea and Nathan
and my grandchildren, Ambur and Mathew*

A Note From the Cover Artist:

My Cosmic Grandmother

She comes from the stars, and I came from her. She was sent here with otherworldly wisdom and a heart that breaks at people's suffering. She gives her hands to the tending of flowers, fruit. and herbs; she relentlessly helps collect household items for the poor; she counsels the hurt; she has led tours to, and written about, sacred sites of the world. When I was born, they did not put me into the arms of my scared fifteen-year-old mother—I was placed in a metal pan and left alone; alone until my grandmother walked over to introduce herself.

Since that first conversation, she has spoken countless wisdoms to me, which I have urged her to write. People often ask me how I didn't end up "messed up" from a crazy, rocky life—I tell them it's because of her. To which she replies, "Oh, I just helped the roses grow." And that she did, through my growing pains and seasons. Her lessons have been passed on to my friends through me, and so I urged her to write them down.

This painting (the artwork is painted completely with nail polish) is for the book I urged her to write, "Cosmic Grandmother Wisdom." Now the seeds of her wild, sometimes unconventional wisdom are here, in this book, to scatter into your hands.

Contents

—m—

You, Me, and the Council of Elders

—✦—

Things I say may not feel right or true to you. That's okay. What is true for one person may not be true for another. Through decades of evaluating, collecting information, questioning and noticing, I've discerned there is no truth with a capital T. No reality with a capital R. We each are working out our own paths and seeking our own truths. I am here to encourage you, to tell you stories you may relate to, to be of any help I can be. I am your equal, not ahead of or above you. We are here on the path through life together. We are family. Hopefully we're friends.

I've lived in this earthly body since 1947. I began hearing the voices of the Council of Elders when I was five, after a near-death experience. I intuited there is a "group"—I lovingly refer to them as The Guys. One of the Elders acts as spokesperson for the entire group. Yuan played that role from when I was fifteen to twenty-three years old. Then Babaji took over for decades. In March 2012 Metatron became spokesperson. I'm aware of at least four other Council members who don't speak directly to me: a Native American male; a dark-haired woman; Jesus' grandmother Anne; and my ascended master self. I intuit there are six altogether.

My Council of Elders has traveled my entire lifetime with me, starting when I was five years old, guiding, encouraging, teaching, analyzing, and helping me to stay aware. Explaining when I got confused. Loving me when I was scared or sad. They are my dear friends.

I also began remembering past lives at the same young age. I called them my "Other Lives." When I was nine years old, my Aunt Edna gave me books to read on Edgar Cayce, T. Lobsang Rampa, and *The Life and Teachings of the Masters of the Far East.* "Other people believe this and there are words for it," I joyfully repeated to myself. "Reincarnation. Karma."

My past lives count is now up to around ninety-seven. I often meet people whom I had known before in another life, and I generally recognize them right away. Often these relationships are difficult, while I learn how to harmonize and balance past debts with each of them. By about age fifteen, I realized I was psychic in other ways also. I was able to read for other people, tell them about their past, present, and future, as well as their own past lives.

Generally, human beings grow what I call "a filter," which seems to be fully in place by the time we're about five to seven years old. This filter keeps us from remembering who and what we are, where we've been, and can also limit psychic communication and information. This filter is important for two reasons. The first is to help us live and learn in present time, what Eckhart Tolle calls the Now. And the other is so that we don't become insane.

For me, the filter never formed properly. (My partner of twenty-three years, Paul, who was a psychological counselor, further explained that I don't have a strong ego.) Part of the reason I wasn't able to fully from a filter was because I arranged to be born into a family who abused and molested me.

It worked!

Because of those experiences, my psychic antenna grew very big and highly sensitive, so that I became attuned to stations not often picked up by earthly beings until recently, as humans are evolving into a new species. More on that later.

I also planned on finishing up ALL my lifetimes on earth, complete my karma, and harmonize all my relationships. I decided I would be a healer. I came into this life with less than the usual amount of energy and health, so I've been sick, tired, and disabled most of my life. It's called the Wounded Healer Syndrome. Perhaps you've heard of it.

I'm not complaining, just explaining how I set up my life and experiences. It was important that I would remember in order to heal what needed to be healed. I came here to learn unconditional love, forgiveness, and gratitude. It has taken me most of my life to accomplish that.

I want you to know that I am NOT an expert on anything—except perhaps suffering. Because I was quiet and in bed a lot, I became contemplative. Yet I'm a Scorpio, so I experience everything quite intensely.

I'm like a bulldog when I'm trying to understand something, especially if it is a mystery or hidden from view. I have a scientific bent, so I study and do my own experiments to see if something works. When I'm satisfied, it becomes one of "Lauren's Laws." I'll explain that in greater detail in another article. I'm not enlightened or awakened, although it's my goal to become so. I did experience about two weeks of awakening in May 2011, which was like going to heaven. But it disappeared and I only get tantalizing glimpses of being awakened from time to time.

I apparently first became acquainted with the Elders in Lemuria (also known as Mu), about 200,000 years ago. Lemuria was our first almost-physical incarnation on this planet. We had a very spiritual society until the continent began to split apart and sink into the ocean.

I can only tell you what I remember. It's like recalling something from long ago. Can you remember experiences from your childhood or adolescence? My memories feel like that. How do I do it? I just *know* stuff. Paul tells me I'm not schizophrenic, if that helps at all!

Therefore, The Guys are also Lemurian Elders, except for Metatron, who is an Archangel. They have no physical, 3-D bodies.

I must be the slow one, because I'm still working on an earthly life. I can converse with them as easily as I do with someone on the telephone or my partner Paul, only telepathically. They don't interfere, and let me learn things on my own. If I'm confused, they explain. Sometimes they'll confirm what I've picked up. Or if I missed something, like when I'm doing a psychic reading, I'll hear them add their own words. If I need to pay attention, they'll alert me. They've taught me how to meditate, how to lucidly dream, how to do psychic readings and healings, and much more. I don't know what I would have done without them.

One final word on the Elders. I read *Destiny of Souls* by Dr. Michael Newton, who used to perform life between lives hypnosis. After working with thousands of people, he came up with a general description on the Council of Elders. When a person dies and goes to the spirit realm, he/she is greeted by a personal guide, then his/her own family of souls. At some point the person goes to see their Council of Elders, who helps the person understand what he/she learned or didn't learn in the past life. The Council members are highly advanced beings, loving, wise, and helpful. A soul will return again and again to their Council after each life, so they are familiar with each other. Just before the soul is ready to return to a new life, he/she meets with the Council again to determine what would be the best choice of lives and what is desired to learn.

According to Dr. Newton's research, every soul has a Guide who helps throughout one's life. However, I've had the entire Council with me these sixty-six years. Why is that? They tell me it's for two reasons:

1. Because I'm now in training to become an Elder
2. Because I'm a Conduit (see the chapter, "Are You a Conduit?")

They work with me very closely. It's hard for me to believe—I don't expect you to believe, either. But that's what they tell me.

An Awakening—The Gift

When I experience a burst of awakening, as I've had the good fortune to experience a few times in my life, I notice my thoughts are like flickering kaleidoscopes of musing. Not important to gather up or focus on or study, they come and go like ice skaters on a smooth rink, twirling and zooming over the unbroken surface, with only tiny glistening shavings to mark where they have been. Then melt into nothingness. As I shift into higher vibrations, a more harmonious consciousness, I realize thoughts don't mean anything. My thoughts float like butterflies in the springtime sun, lovely and ephemeral, sipping nectar from fragrant flowers. Momentarily savoring the sweetness, then wafting away.

Rather than thoughts, it's feelings that move me to action or a gentle hammock-like swaying of contentment. When I need to accomplish something, an urge arises like a soap bubble from the void, the field of all possibilities, the divine matrix. In that moment, I attend and the job is done quickly. Effortlessly. And then the accomplishment fades back into the void, to dissolve and later reassemble its particles into a different desire.

I don't have to do anything when I'm in an awakened state. Neither fight nor flight—but simply float. I'm in a different perspective where life puts on new dresses and models its countless vistas. I'm interested and curious from the vantage point of happiness, peace, and joy. I vaguely remember how I used to make myself upset.

Nothing is serious in that state of being. I laugh at most stories and dramas, not because I'm unkind but because I am joyful. The power of joy can and does change difficult situations because joy sees through a different set of eyes. The Elders have told me recently that my happiness is the greatest gift I can give the world.

I notice my own and others' forgiveness as though an outbreak of unconditional love has mutated into a viral contagion. Ethics, too, have elbowed their way into human dialogue and action. No longer does might make right. Power is no longer to the fittest—but the finest.

Even writing is not important, only that I want to write. And enjoy. It's like strolling through a forest glade of the mind, filled with awe and delight at the words that appear to me. A juggler with her idea-balls.

Away from my former struggling nights, life is effortless and fun. All animosities melt like snowdrifts in a warm dawn, replaced by gratitude and a hug.

Awakening exists in the now. No destination but the excitement of experiencing new levels of happiness and quiet creativity. The gift is to feel ease, to dissolve burdens and concerns. To soar free like a red-tailed hawk on the thermal currents, above the earth yet still connected to it.

I fill whole notebooks with what I want. In an awakened state, I don't want anything but what I have and what I am. Peaceful. Happy. Content. I lick the chocolate ice-cream cone of life; its sweetness lingers on my tongue.

I weep in joy. My heart explodes. Light surges everywhere in the cosmos with the Gift. I look forward to more.

Miraculous!
What to Do If a Police Officer Stops You

———✍︎———

I recently was pulled over by a policeman because I was inadvertently speeding (36 in a 20 mph zone). I was very happy that day and not paying attention to my driving through a school zone. In other words, I was driving through La-La Land instead of being grounded!

I was shocked out of my reverie when I saw the flashing lights show up in my rear-view mirror and the piercing, unmistakable sound of a siren. I pulled over quickly, my heart pounding.

When the very young police officer came to my window, I smiled and said, "Hi." I wasn't scared or angry, but felt quite loving, although somewhat disoriented.

"I'm sorry, Ma'am. You were going 36 mph in a school zone, which is posted at 20 mph." His demeanor seemed almost apologetic.

"That's okay, my dear," I replied. "You're just doing your job," and smiled at him. I inexplicably felt tender towards him. Not at all upset.

"Could I see your driver's license and registration?" he asked gently.

"Of course." I got out my license and fumbled around in the glove compartment. I came out with a wad of papers and went through all of them. "Here's my registration. But I don't seem to find my current car insurance. I do have insurance. See, here's the bill." I felt idiotic. "The amount is taken out every month from my bank account," I continued.

He waved my concern away. "That's okay," he replied.

Then the young officer returned to his car, to contact headquarters to make sure the car wasn't stolen, and I wasn't a criminal on the lam.

Although I was calm, my body felt agitated. I notice that my body has a "mind" of its own. I decided to meditate while I waited.

As I meditated I asked my Council of Elders if I deserved a ticket. If I did, I would pay it without complaint, surrendering to the Universe. I had been, after all, speeding.

But if being pulled over was just a wake-up call, that was fine. If the message was simply for me to "pay attention," I got the message loud and clear. Meanwhile I felt very detached to the outcome.

After quite a long wait, the police officer returned to my car.

"I couldn't get my computer to work," he apologized. "For some reason the computer just stopped operating, which is why it took me so long. I can't write you a ticket. I'm letting you go with a warning. Be sure to pay attention in the future." He handed me back my paperwork.

"Thank you so much, darling," I replied. (Darling??) "I will. And you have a wonderful day!"

As I drove off, I thanked the Elders for the warning, giggling to myself about the police officer's computer.

What the Universe can do amazes me! And what love and surrender can do amazes me, too!!

The Importance of
Psychic/Spiritual Discernment

—⚬⚬—

Lately I feel disturbed, as though our world has decided to become a genuine Tower of Babel. Not with a multitude of languages but an overwhelming spewing of beliefs—with each person seeming to think that his or her belief is the only accurate one. And there is a battle of these beliefs, encouraging others to engage in battle. The battle creates war, frightening or separating or polarizing each other into not just two warring camps but many.

I recognize it in my own family. I see it on Facebook and elsewhere on the internet. I hear it on TV and the radio. I want to run far away, hide myself from the roar of righteous discord, and bury myself in something non-contentious. How do I know who— if any—are right?

Perhaps the most important facet of anyone's life is to be able to determine messages of guidance from a superior source, to know one's personal truth. One could call that source a Conscience, a Higher Self, the Universe, Intuition, Guides, God, Jesus Christ, Allah, angels or any other life-affirming being. Whatever its name, without it, one is destined to struggle through life's labyrinth, lost and bereft of direction, without guidance, bewildered or fearful. That guidance I call psychic/spiritual discernment.

The **Guidance of Discernment** comes in various forms, similar to our human senses:

Feeling (clairsentience)

Hearing (clairaudience)

Seeing (clairvoyance)

Tasting (clairgustance)

Smelling (clairalience) This one is not very well developed in most people, although I think it may be working when we are not paying much attention. Like being able to "sniff out" a situation. Or something "smells" fishy. Scientists have discovered that a couple cannot mate or stay together without literally "smelling okay" to each other.

We can possess one or more of these systems, and can develop each with conscious practice.

I believe we are born with these abilities. Studies have shown that even fetuses in utero can discern the mother and/or its outside environment.

Noticing and Awareness/ Paying Attention—The first step in development and working with your personal source field is to notice. Notice when you get a message. This may be quiet or loud, a little prickle of conscience or a smack on the head with a 2 x 4, a huge picture or a tiny cartoon, a small event or a large disaster. You could keep a journal of what is noticed, which helps to develop even more awareness.

Trusting What You Get—Many people don't trust their intuitive messages. Your logical mind can chalk it up to overactive imagination, wishful thinking, lack of sleep, or simply making it up. Just allow yourself to trust, for now. Wait and watch. Sometimes it may take a while to realize you are right. Once in a while you may get no confirmation, but keep trusting anyway. Trusting will "build" your intuitive muscles.

Act On It—if you pay attention to your message and take action—doing or refraining from doing—and pay attention to what happens next, you may be surprised at the accuracy or validity of the message.

Your Message is Specifically For You – No one else may get your message. That doesn't mean it's wrong, just personal. Picture in your mind Creator/Source as a giant computer, connected to the entire cosmos of existence through software planted in each of our beings. And you may not resonate with anyone else's message either. Pay attention to that!

Visualize this—A vision presented itself to me about twelve years ago. I saw each person on earth, their energy fields appearing like separate cornucopias floating in space. The message was that every person is living in his/her own unique universe, in which everything in that universe is "true."

That means that there is no one truth, with a capital T, just relative truth. Each separate universe (person) has its own particular truth that is connected to discernment for that individual and for that individual's path through life.

My Council of Elders has explained that everyone's main job in life is to learn, grow, and evolve. Sometimes we learn through positive actions, sometimes negative ones. And we have limitless lifetimes to perfect those lessons.

Each lesson is designed to enrich our soul's development, as well as to learn through participation in the entire world's lessons. Therefore, a Mother Teresa is just as important as a Saddam Hussein, regardless of how he or she may impact us directly or indirectly.

The Elders say "everything is perfect, no matter what it looks like." Without discernment we cannot follow our own path. Life on Earth is not a crap shoot, but a carefully, deliberately, lovingly orchestrated jigsaw puzzle of events and people, intended for each soul to grow and learn more evolved and spiritual lessons.

We are not human beings having a spiritual experience. We are spiritual beings having human experiences. And with each experience we have free will, to choose or not, to feel or not, to respond or not, to learn or not.

My Council of Elders tells me that living in our holographic universe is like living on a spider web of existence.

One Person Can Make a Difference—Because that action vibrates the spider web. As scientists have discovered, if you change one tiny aspect of a hologram, the entire hologram changes.

I grew up in a household where I was abused and molested by both parents and an uncle. My soul deliberately chose this scenario in order for me to learn forgiveness, compassion, and finally gratitude. It wasn't easy. It has taken the better part of my adult life to learn these things – and not just for the perpetrators of personal crimes against me as a little child, but towards all perpetrators living and dead, for whom my growth into forgiveness and gratitude affects the entire world.

Practice—the more you practice, the better at discerning you will get. I trust myself and my personal messages more than anything else or anyone else in the world, although sometimes I forget.

The difficulty today is not simply discerning our own path and rightness of action, but of others and the world. We are bombarded with a dizzying plethora of stories from one extreme to the other. I've heard so much. I'm sure you have, too, such as:

- Corporate news media and their nighttime bad news
- Stories of global warming, the pollution and loss of air, water, land, food, the death of millions of people and species worldwide
- Vitriolic bashing of political opponents on all sides
- Reports of legislation that removes our Bill of Rights
- Stories of an Illuminati cabal preparing to take over our world. enslave us and murder nine-tenths of us
- Stories of awakening, ascension, and enlightenments

- Stories of secret forces in the Pentagon and military preparing to free us from corporate and political domination
- Russian scientists decoding of crop circles warning of five impending disasters that will destroy Earth
- Extreme events on Earth and extreme solar events
- Stories of hatred, despair, violence, unceasing wars, repressions

I'm not implying you must remain passive, unless that is what you discern is appropriate for you. I am saying that if you feel "inspired" to take a particular action, TRUST and ACT upon it. There is no wrong action, only inaction if action is what inspires you or vice-versa. And even if you take a supposed "wrong" action or no action, you will learn from that, too. In other words, you can't lose!

I've had my own personal messages about myself within the world as it exists today. I am generally peaceful, because my personal message that I discern is: "I'm fine. Nothing to be worried about." Yours will be exclusive to you. I encourage you to PRACTICE.

Knowledge is Power—Except When It Isn't

We can't solve problems by using the same kind of thinking we used when we created them."—Albert Einstein

I was napping. Then in early January, 2003 President Bush helped me wake up. Thus I became an activist in the lead-up to the Iraqi occupation. I protested with friends every Friday on Hemet's main street in front of Denny's until September 2003. I began researching and discovered shocking details about our government; money and power brokers; the media; politics; 9-11; defense contractors; peak oil and other natural resources; global problems; corruption; and greed. I published a weekly online newsletter detailing what I was discovering. I continued my research for the next seven years. I was always angry, depressed or scared.

I joined activism and protest groups, many which had been around since the Vietnam War. Together we took many actions. Paul and I participated in the L.A. demonstration in February 2003—the famous world-wide mass protests with hundreds of millions of people joined against attacking Iraq. We all "knew" there were no WMD's and that the so-called war was a smoke screen for a hidden agenda. Boy, was I mad at Colin Powell for his dog-and-pony show at the U.N! He didn't look too happy either, and afterwards he disappeared from public view.

After a few futile years these groups began to disband. We seemingly had no President or Congress. We "knew" from the election of 2000 that the Supreme Court could be bought off. The media seemed to cover news stories that furthered the power brokers' agenda. Some people were getting rich from the take-over in Iraq while both our countries suffered.

Paul and I sold all our holdings and moved to Whidbey Island, Washington to create a survival farm. I expected terrible events to befall us all.

I "knew" gas prices would skyrocket before they did. I "knew" the housing market bubble would burst two years before it actually did. I "knew" our economy would falter. I saw our planet ravaged by uncontrollable forces, species going extinct, human existence in question.

My friends didn't want to talk to me anymore. I couldn't understand. Didn't they want to know what was going on? After all, knowledge is power, right? But did it matter what I knew? Did what I know, or believe I knew, change anything?

In 2009 Michael Ruppert came out with his movie, *Collapse,* a documentary about the coming collapse of our society. Shortly afterwards he created a website, *CollapseNet.com.* I wrote articles for his website and continued researching. I read what others were saying on Ruppert's website. One gentle psychologist, who wrote a series of articles on how to cope with economic collapse, went out and bought a gun! *A gun?* In the event of total collapse, if people came to our farm, desperate for food or shelter, how could I possibly shoot them? The answer was I couldn't. I wouldn't. Besides which, how many guns would it take to protect us? How much ammunition? I would need an army. No, I wasn't going to go in that direction. I'd invite whoever showed up to stay. I'd feed them. We were already storing thousands of dollars of food, seed, and other essentials. I'd teach them how to grow food and raise chickens.

Then a reader posed a question to me. What if 200 people showed up at our farm? 2,000 people? What then?

I began to question my whole premise of knowing as much as I could.

The whole fabric of my debate unraveled. I was left with a great, empty unknowing. I simply didn't know anything!

Fortunately at that point I began to have miraculous experiences. A divine hand removed all my fear. I experienced Oneness Blessings. I practiced Divine Openings. We sold our farm, gave away all the items we had stored, and moved to a quiet little neighborhood. I started experiencing profound awakenings. I saw life from a completely different perspective—because my consciousness was shifting into something completely different. My outer life began to change. I began to experience causeless bliss. I was happy, no matter what the external world was doing.

So I return to my original premise. Is knowledge really power? Whose knowledge? Can we truly know anything? I think it may depend on the specific knowledge. Or perhaps it is subject to the mindset assimilating that knowledge. Maybe there's only relative truth. Perhaps we are evolving from knowledge into wisdom. I don't know.

There are two charts that come to mind as I consider these questions. The first is an excerpt from Dr. David Hawkins' book, *Power vs. Force*.

God-view	Life-view	Level	Log	Emotion	Process
Self	Is	**ENLIGHTENMENT**	700-1000	Ineffable	Pure Consciousness
All-Being	Perfect	**PEACE**	600	Bliss	Illumination
One	Complete	**JOY**	540	Serenity	Transfiguration
Loving	Benign	**LOVE**	500	Reverence	Revelation
Wise	Meaningful	**REASON**	400	Understanding	Abstraction
Merciful	Harmonious	**ACCEPTANCE**	350	Forgiveness	Transcendence
Inspiring	Hopeful	**WILLINGNESS**	310	Optimism	Intention
Enabling	Satisfactory	**NEUTRALITY**	250	Trust	Release
Permitting	Feasible	**COURAGE turning point**	200	Affirmation	Empowerment
Indifferent	Demanding	**PRIDE**	175	Scorn	Inflation
Vengeful	Antagonistic	**ANGER**	150	Hate	Aggression
Denying	Disappointing	**DESIRE**	125	Craving	Enslavement
Punitive	Frightening	**FEAR**	100	Anxiety	Withdrawal
Disdainful	Tragic	**GRIEF**	75	Regret	Despondency
Condemning	Hopeless	**APATHY**	50	Despair	Abdication
Vindictive	Evil	**GUILTY**	30	Blame	Destruction
Despising	Miserable	**SHAME**	20	Humiliation	Elimination

According to Dr. Hawkins, the higher the emotion on the chart, the more power one has. I was struck by the idea that I could make more of a difference by staying home and being peaceful, than by demonstrating or judging or blaming.

A second chart (below) is from Carl Calleman in his study of the sacred Mayan Calendar of evolution. His chart shows the evolution of consciousness in nine stages (the Mayans called them Underworlds), beginning with the Big Bang 16.4 billion years ago through October 28, 2011, when all nine stages coalesce. "The prophetic Mayan calendar is not keyed to the movement of planetary bodies. Instead, it functions as a metaphysical map of the evolution of consciousness and records how spiritual time flows – providing a new science of time…the Mayan calendar is a spiritual device that enables a greater understanding of the evolution of consciousness driving human history and the concrete steps we can take to align ourselves with this growth toward enlightenment."[1] Dates correspond closely with scientific findings.

Universal (ninth)	Evolution of cosmic consciousness	Conscious co-creation	Feb. 11, 2011– Oct. 28, 2011
Galactic (eighth)	Evolution of galactic consciousness	Ethics	Jan. 5, 1999– Oct. 28, 2011
Planetary (seventh)	Evolution of global consciousness	Power	July 24, 1755– Oct. 28, 2011
National (sixth)	Evolution of civilized consciousness	Laws & Punishment	Aug. 11, 3115– Oct. 28, 2011
Regional (fifth)	Evolution of human consciousness	Complex tools, language, art	100,000 BC– Oct. 28, 2011
Tribal (fourth)	Evolution of hominid consciousness	First humans	2 million BC– Oct. 28, 2011
Familial (third)	Evolution of anthropoid consciousness	First primates	40 million BC– Oct. 28, 2011
Mammal (second)	Evolution mammalian consciousness	First animals	850 million BC– Oct. 28, 2011
Cellular (first)	Evolution of cellular consciousness	Big bang, galaxies, stars, higher cells	16.4 billion yrs.- Oct. 28, 2011

Why should this concern me, you ask? What difference does it make if I'm living here in my own little world, doing what I do? I'm not hurting anyone.

David Bohm, a physicist and Einstein's protégé, would beg to differ. He culminated his brilliant career with the conclusion: "Everything is connected to everything." Jung referred to it as the collective unconscious. Rupert Sheldrake named it the morphic resonance field. Lynn McTaggert calls it simply The Field. Gregg Braden names it the Divine Matrix. Quantum physicists talk about reality as consisting only of vibrational and energetic probabilities.

In other words, on the level of consciousness, vibration, and energy, we are all in this together. Whatever one of us feels (feeling is vibration and energy) affects the whole.

The good news is, according to Dr. Hawkins, if some of us elevate our emotions to the top quarter of the chart, we can affect our planet in a powerfully positive way. Experiments of this kind were done in the 1970's, called the Maharishi effect, which "defined as the influence of coherence and positivity in the social and natural environment."[2] The numbers on Hawkins' chart are logarithmic, similar to the power of earthquakes. "An earthquake that measures 5.0 on the Richter scale has shaking amplitude 10 times larger and corresponds to an energy release of $\sqrt{1000} \approx 31.6$ times greater than one that measures 4.0."[3] Therefore, neutrality is more than 2.5 times as powerful than fear; love is 10 times more powerful than apathy, and so on.

As of October 28, 2011, according to Calleman, we have arrived at the highest period of human evolution since the Big Bang—conscious co-creation. Is it possible that focusing on what is wrong with the world perpetuates what is wrong? Maybe it is time for us to utilize the power of higher vibrational emotions, coupled with the power of co-creating what we DO want.

Maybe that will be the evolving "knowledge" that is truly power.

[1] *Calleman.com*

[2] *http://www.mum.edu/m_effect/*

[3] *Wikipedia.com (earthquake)*

The Complete Idiot's Guide to Enlightenment From Suffering to Bliss in Two Steps

—∞—

Such as are thy habitual thoughts, such also will be the character of thy mind; for the soul is dyed by the thoughts—Marcus Aurelius

My lifelong desire has always been to become enlightened and be at peace. I lived a life of fear, suffering, chronic fatigue and fibromyalgia, PTSD, depression, anxieties, agitation, phobias, and loneliness. I spent well over $200,000 trying to get well and achieve happiness. I learned so many traditional and non-traditional medical modalities that I wrote a book to share that information (*Alternatives for Everyone*, 1988).

Nothing much helped. Until recently.

My change consists of two parts, linked in important ways. I learned Part 1 from Lola Jones (*Divine Openings.com*; "Things are Going Great in My Absence.") I learned that life was simply comprised of emotions and thoughts—that is what we call reality. To change your reality, to awaken and become enlightened, you must fully FEEL emotions—**Part 1** and LET GO of thoughts—**Part 2**. Here's how:

PART 1—EMOTIONS

1. Pay attention to what emotion you are feeling
2. Locate the emotion on Emotions Chart** (just notice)
3. Feel that emotion fully, without judgment or stories
4. Invite Divine Energy (God, higher self, universe, field of probabilities) into yourself
5. Ask Divine Energy to shift to that emotion higher up on the chart
6. Feel the shift upward. (This could take seconds, hours, days, or longer. Be patient. The emotion is all-important.)
7. Thank Divine Energy for the upward shift, no matter how small the shift might have been

Regardless of the level of the emotion you are feeling, you can always move higher.

You can practice Part 1 any time you are experiencing an unpleasant or unwanted emotional level.

Part 1 was very helpful but, for me, incomplete. Traumatic early childhood experiences combined with my being highly verbal created overwhelming torturous thoughts, against which I felt helpless. I began to notice that when these thoughts surfaced, I went down to the bottom of the emotional scale into a virtual "hell." I discovered that I, like many of us, had become an assemblage of unhelpful stories. With some insight and practice, I created Part 2.

You may find it helpful to practice Part 1 until you can clearly feel and identify distinct emotions, and then practice Part 2.

PART 2 – THOUGHTS

1. Recognize a thought that brings you down on the emotion chart and feels unpleasant. (e.g. My husband doesn't pay attention to me; The economy is getting worse; If only my child would do what I say; What if I lose my job; My father is disappointed in me; My neighbor

---

** The Emotions Chart is located towards the end of this article.

is noisy; I don't like my body.)

2. Reframe that thought as an "unhelpful story." (Stories can be factual or not. The point is whether or not the story is unhelpful, that is, if it brings an unpleasant emotion.)

3. Bring your awareness to it and say / think to yourself, "This is an unhelpful story."

4. Observe as the story disappears. Once a story is recognized, it usually dissolves immediately. My metaphor for this is: "Shine a flashlight on a cockroach and it scuttles away."

5. Continue to recognize "unhelpful stories" as they appear in your awareness. Bring your awareness to each and EVERY one and say/think to yourself, "This is an unhelpful story." Observe as the story disappears.

6. If a particular story doesn't immediately disappear, repeat "This is an unhelpful story" until it does. (I found old, ingrained stories sometimes took up to three repetitions before disappearing.)

7. A VACUUM or VOID is created in the absence of the unhelpful story. The Void grows as you continue to "disappear" unhelpful stories. It feels like you are vacuuming your consciousness!

You don't need to fight an unhelpful story for it to disappear. All that is required is to bring your awareness to each one.

THAT'S IT! All you need to do is Feel your emotions and Discount your thoughts.

These two exercises above, when practiced regularly, can take you to living at the top of the Emotions Chart—happiness, love, contentment, bliss, ecstasy—Enlightenment.

Where do unhelpful stories come from and where do they go? Shree Bhagavan, an Awakened person who created the Oneness University in India says, "The mind is not mine. There are thoughts but no thinker."

Shark Attacks: If you are ever bombarded by a rowdy bunch of unhelpful stories (I call these "shark attacks"), you can bring awareness to each one, or you can imagine you have a "laser gun of awareness" and disappear them all at once.

One Word Unhelpful Stories: Sometimes unhelpful stories can consist of just one word: "Fat, ugly, old, poor, can't, hate, etc.." I believe there can be an entire unhelpful story attached to a single word. Repeat Part 2.

Physical Sensations: Sometimes unhelpful stories can surround a physical sensation: pain or discomfort anywhere, bloating, tiredness, sickness or disease of any kind. (I found many unhelpful stories were attached to symptoms of my chronic fatigue and fibromyalgia.) Repeat Part 2 as if the physical sensation was an unhelpful story, focusing on what may be attached to the sensation. Don't focus on the sensation itself, but just slightly outside of it.

Endless Loop Stories: An unhelpful story can become an endless loop, repeating until I bring my awareness to it and disappear it. For example: "I have a headache. I have a headache. I have a headache." Repeat Part 2.

Unhelpful Stories Seem More Numerous When:
- Thinking about the past
- Thinking about the future
- Residing in lower than "Acceptance" on the Emotions Chart.
- Experiencing pain or sickness
- Listening to others' unhelpful stories.
- The higher on the Emotions Chart, the fewer and less persistent unhelpful stories emerge. I notice that when I'm stabilized on a higher level of emotion, I experience far fewer thoughts of any kind.

Other People's Unhelpful Stories: (friends, family, news, movies, TV, books, magazines, teachers, doctors) can affect me the same way my own unhelpful stories do. I can silently notice the unhelpful story and follow the same steps in Part 2.

Or I can explain to the person what I'm doing (Part 2) and so share this method.

Or I can laugh. I have discovered that laughing disappears the stories, while stabilizing me on the emotion level I prefer, often joy. Spontaneous laughter is something that is recently emerging, so I am still experimenting.

Or I can implement Part 1 and shoot up into a higher emotional level.

A Particular Story Takes Me To A Specific Emotion (if left unnoticed): Angry stories take me to anger. Sad stories take me to sorrow. Judgmental stories take me to judgment, etc. An unhelpful story resonates to a particular emotion. It is my experience that an unhelpful story shows up just a nanosecond before the emotion is experienced. Buddhism teaches that thoughts create suffering. Now I know how.

Comparisons (both favorable and unfavorable) are unhelpful stories. Notice the unhelpful stories: ("He's bigger, richer, smarter, taller than me" or "He's poorer, dumber, shorter than me") and follow the steps in Part 2.

Should a Helpful Story be Used Instead? No. I find that these (like affirmations) don't reach the depths or ignite the lasting changes that this method does, because with this method a void is created that is filled with positive energy by the universe.

Should a Helpful Story be Put into the Place Vacated by an Unhelpful Story? No. Although helpful stories are an improvement over unhelpful ones, stories still have limitations. I want to stay limitless and so opt for the universe to fill the void for me (the universe hates a vacuum). The void left by disappearing unhelpful stories is filled with the immensely positive energy of the universe.

I Discovered Different Types of Thoughts:

- Helpful stories and Unhelpful stories
- Memo—Go to bed. Eat breakfast. Call my sister. Walk the dog. $E=mc^2$.
- Messages from a divine source

Wondrous Benefits I've Noticed:

I think these come about because a different emotional state has a different vibration. Reality is vibration. Hence higher emotions vibrate differently. Positive emotions and outcomes occur oftener, last longer, and are felt more deeply.

- Stabilizing in upper emotions—e.g. peace, contentment, happiness, love, bliss, ecstasy
- Spontaneous, joyful laughter
- Relationships evolving into more positive ones; more friends and more fun
- Changing the outward state of my life
- Enjoying the benefits of a meditative state without meditating
- Dissolving the past and suffering
- Dissolving melodramas
- Experiencing more synchronicities and miracles
- Shifting into a state of awakening and enlightenment

The Emotions Chart

Ecstasy, Joy, Bliss
Knowing, Empowerment
Freedom
Love, Appreciation, Gratitude
Passion, Eagerness, Enthusiasm
Happiness, Positive Expectation
Optimism, Confidence, I Can Do It
Hopefulness, Seeing Possibilities, Curiosity
Self-Esteem, Interest, Courage
Contentment, Relaxation, Emptiness
Acceptance, Boredom, Don't Care—This is a resting zone; above the line is worthiness
Pessimism, I Give Up
Frustration, Aggravation, Impatience—__THE TIPPING POINT__
Overwhelm, Stressed, Hard Work—much of society lives here and thinks it's normal
Disappointment,   Doubt, Confusion, Uncertainty
Worry, Negative Expectation
Discouragement, Quit, Fatigue
Anger—A bridge to get your power/energy back
Revenge, Hatred, Rage, Jealousy, Desire that feels bad, Lack
Guilt, Blame, Projection on Others, Fear
Sadness, Grief, Depression
Shame, Unworthiness, Despair, Apathy; Death.

*** *(chart courtesy of Lola Jones, www.divineopenings.com)*

The Universal Bank Account

—⚭—

The Universal Bank Account is not just about money I recognized early in my life that the universe has an explicit connection between "giving" and "receiving." The connection is like a revolving door, similar to Sir Isaac Newton's law of motion: for every action there is an equal and opposite reaction. I call it the Universal Bank Account.

Simply put: When a person gives, the universe is then obligated to give back, to return energy to the sender, or else the universe would become unbalanced. The person receives from the universe. It only appears that a person receives from someone or something else. But in truth it is the universe giving back (through whatever means at its disposal).

The most wonderful part of this dual motion is that the energy the universe sends to the original person may not show up immediately. That energy goes into what I call the Universal Bank Account. Then when that same person needs something at a future date—money, a job, help fixing a tire, friendliness, a hug—the universe supplies it, withdrawing energy from that person's Universal Bank Account. Energy moves in an endless loop—a cycle for each individual—through giving, then receiving, giving and receiving. Into infinity.

I've been questioned by skeptics on my theory. What I tell them is this: Don't take my word for it. Try it yourself. Experiment.

Since I'm not a trained scientist I may have explained my theory badly. So I will simply explain how to do it, and then you can experiment for yourself.

Everyday—give something. Many somethings. As many somethings as you can think of. You could give money to someone who needs it—a friend, relative, neighbor, a stranger, or a charity. You could buy groceries for someone or give food to the food bank. You could feed wild birds or animals. You could help clean up pollution. You could recycle. You could save energy by turning out lights or bicycling or any other method.

Giving could also be more ephemeral, like smiling at a stranger. Giving someone your place in line at the check-out counter. Volunteering to help in any way. Letting traffic go by on a busy street. Pulling weeds from a disabled person's lawn. Writing articles for free.

There is a myriad of giving you can do. Most of it does not necessitate money. All giving requires is a smidgen of awareness and a desire (even a miniscule desire) to give.

ALL of that giving goes directly into your Universal Bank Account. When you need something, that something will simply show up without muss or fuss, sometimes miraculously! It's merely a withdrawal from your account, paid by the universe. You can understand that you may want to keep filling up your account.

LACK OF GIVING—I have seen people who are in need yet nothing shows up. No miracles. Just struggle. When I have examined their lives more closely, I see that they are not giving. Their Universal Bank Account is overdrawn.

When someone in need asks me what he/she can do to improve his/her lot in life, I say GIVE! And give. And give. And give some more! When that person does so, his/her life turns around dramatically, mysteriously, magically, sometimes instantly. I have seen this many times and I haven't seen it fail yet.

LACK OF RECEIVING—A popular saying from religion is that "it is better to give than receive." I disagree. One must do both. I have noticed people who are good at giving, but have difficulty receiving. When they need something, often nothing shows up—because they are not open to it. One must be able to give and receive, otherwise the cycle gets clogged and the Universal Bank Account system doesn't operate properly. When I am with a person who is having difficulty receiving whatever I am giving (a compliment, a present, whatever)—I tell them "Just say thank you." What a non-receiving person fails to understand is that to refusing to receive is an insult to the giver. If you are one of those non-receivers, just practice saying thank you. That's all it takes.

SPIRITUAL—Several of my friends have questioned me on this theory, about whether it was "spiritual" or not. They're worried I'm manipulating the universe. I tell them: "Giving and receiving is the active universe. I just notice and play its wonderful pastime. What I do is intrinsically spiritual." When people tithe at church, they expect it to be multiplied back to them.

DIVIDENDS—I've given much during my lifetime. Whenever someone wanted to repay me (who usually couldn't) I told that person to "pass it on." Give that amount to someone else who needs it. In fact, I prefer it. My reasoning is if a person is going to repay me, say, $100, I would rather the universe deposit it in my bank account. Because I'll get a much BIGGER return than just $100. I'll get what I actually need, which generally is much more than the original $100. I call that extra bonus "dividends."

When my partner Paul and I had a farm, I away gave a lot of food and/or sold it cheaply. Paul complained I wasn't charging enough. I told him it would come back to us—probably multiplied. Considering all the miracles we had on the farm, I would say I was correct, courtesy of the Universal Bank Account.

How to Easily Get What You Want by Writing a God Letter

—✦—

'm not suggesting that you can get what you want. I'm telling you! I've used this method for over forty years and it works fabulously. Whenever I want something new, I sit down and do this process. It's fast and usually takes less than an hour to concoct.

I've called the method my "God Letter"—although you don't need to believe in God or a higher power. You can be an agnostic or atheist and this method will still work great for you. You can call it the "Universe Letter" if you want. One thing we can all agree on is that we live in the universe.

The "God Letter" consists of a few simple steps. Mostly the letter is a brainstorming device, which "e-mails" your request to the "Field of all Possibilities" as Deepak Chopra calls the un-manifested universe. You're going to be manifesting something out of nothing. A little bit like your own personal Big Bang.

Here Are The Steps:

Get out a fresh, whole piece of paper (lined is good) and a pen or pencil, whatever you're comfortable with. Hand-writing is more powerful than typing your letter on the computer. Make your writing legible, neat, and tidy. You want the universe to clearly understand what you are asking to manifest.

1. **Current date** (day/month/year)

2. **Dear Universe:**

3. **I....... (Put your full name here) NOW HAVE the PERFECT........ (Fill in the blank).** This could be a job, car, love relationship, house, apartment, housekeeper, employee, employer, career, vacation, health, enlightenment—or whatever you want. Limit this letter to just one manifestation, though. You can always write more letters.

4. **Details:** (here's where you're going to put your brain, heart, and imagination to work) List every single feature you can think of that would describe your perfect........ (Fill in the blank) Make this list as detailed as possible. Leave nothing out, no matter how far-fetched it seems to you. Forget your logical mind while doing your list. Your list does NOT have to make sense. Your list does not have to be "practical." Put fear on the back-burner. It isn't needed here.

   Don't assume anything. The universe is not a mind-reader. Be specific. Write it down. Include a TARGET DATE—month/day/year. This helps the universe to know when you expect your manifestation. Make your date reasonable. You'll know what that is.

5. After you've finished your very detailed list, you will write these exact words: **"This or something better now manifests for the good of all concerned."**

The reason for this sentence is:

—You don't want to limit yourself to what you have asked for. The universe may want to give you more!

—The word NOW is very potent. Just ask Eckhardt Tolle. Manifestation exists in the NOW.

—The good of all concerned—you don't want to take something away from someone else. This phrase protects your integrity.

—You want the manifestation to be for your own highest good as well as for others.

6. Finish with, "Thank you, God."

Gratitude is a very powerful, spiritual vibration, bringing good things your way. Gratitude is an excellent practice to perform every day.

7. Sign your name the way you wrote it at the top of the letter.

8. Put this letter somewhere where you can see it every day, like on the bathroom mirror or refrigerator. Although you have included a target date, you may receive your manifestation sooner—or later— than you have written. The universe operates with synchronicities, so it has to arrange and orchestrate your manifestation. Relax. The Universe Letter is a process.

I suggest you start with a simple request. This helps you become acquainted with how to do the process and to build your manifestation muscles. Not to mention it will give your skeptical mind something stress-free to work on, and work up to. You may want to write a series of letters. You can then clearly see what you're willing to allow into your life by what shows up! With practice you will be able to manifest with greater ease. At least that's been my experience.

How can you can write a beautifully crafted letter of your own? Primarily with the details on your list.

Let's imagine you want to manifest your perfect apartment. You would answer questions like those below with your list:

Price per month—would that include utilities? How about security deposit? First and last month's rent? Work exchange?—be specific with what YOU want.

Locale—city, state—preferred neighborhoods if you know them—by water, mountains, desert, rural, suburban, cityscape—be specific—what do you WANT?

Size—square footage, one-story, two-story, basement, attic—lot size—age of apartment (Victorian, Art Deco, modern), condition of apartment and neighborhood—if you want an apartment freshly painted, newly carpeted, clean and bright, say that! Be specific. Include the colors of the walls and carpet while you're at it. Do you want a workroom in the garage? Include it.

Amenities—which direction do you want your entrance to face? Windows (sunny or shady)? Number of bedrooms, bathrooms? Size of living room, dining room, kitchen? What kind of cabinetry? Plumbing? Electrical? Appliances? Do you want a fireplace, pool, exercise room, jacuzzi, what kind of landscaping? Bathtub or just shower? Garage? Garage door opener? Furnished or not? All the sinks, tubs, toilets are modern and work perfectly? Be specific.

Extras—such as stained glass windows, French doors, glass chandelier, indirect lighting, modern bathroom lighting, special wallpaper, skylights, whatever you can think of you'd like. Be creative.

Neighbors—close or far away, loving, kind, quiet, helpful, friendly, keep to their own business? Imagine these people in your mind. Remember your past experiences!

What kind of street and neighborhood? Quiet, attractive, tree-lined, safe, free of graffiti, close to shopping, schools, what kind of shopping and schools? What kind of children for your children to play with and be friends with?

How you (and your family) will feel in this apartment—happy, content, energetic, loving, peaceful, and creative? What do you want? And of course include a date for your anticipated move-in.

Do You See You Are Creating a Contract? As If You Were Talking To a Realtor, Lawyer, and a Salesperson? You are! You wouldn't go to a car dealership and merely say "I want to buy a car." You would specify make, model, year, price, extras, financing. You wouldn't call Sears and ask them to send a refrigerator without specifying what you want. You might end up with any old refrigerator. That's the point. You use the same methodology in your

Universe Letter. You are training yourself to WANT what you want and GET what you want. Don't accept pale imitations anymore! Don't just put up with. Don't make do.

You are ordering from the "Sears in the Sky," and you deserve to get what you desire. In fact, the universe wants you to manifest your desires. You and the universe are one!

Over time I manifest about 90% of what I ask for. Sometimes I get 100%.

I figure if I ask for a lot, then the odds are better. Often I will get items I didn't even put in my letter. Those are bonuses. Remember, "this or something better now manifests." As you write down items you want, you may find yourself feeling excited. Your excitement lets you know you are on the right track.

I wouldn't advise you to "try to figure out" how your manifestation will occur. Just trust that the Universe has begun working for you already. In truth, the Universe is always working for you. But this time you have special ordered a specific request, rather than longing for a vague desire. That makes all the difference in the world (cliché intended).

More helpful information:

In the chapter "The Complete Idiot's Guide to Enlightenment (From Suffering to Bliss in Two Parts)" feeling your emotions and disappearing your unhelpful stories focuses more energy into manifestation.

Another chapter I recommend is "The Universal Bank Account," how the Universe operates in giving and receiving. That chapter details how to help "prime the pump" to manifest what you want even more powerfully.

Manifesting a Person or Relationship:

You will need to be very specific. You may want to take a few days to think about and imagine the qualities you are looking for. (Twenty-five years ago I did the God Letter to manifest a boyfriend. He was everything on the list. But, I didn't read the fine print. He had several traits I didn't want—addictions and violent tendencies! Bear in mind that people are very complex.)

You must think like a Divine Attorney, considering the fine print and contractual information.

You must NOT try to manifest a specific person, only qualities that you want in a person. Otherwise the Universe's manifestation will either backfire on you or not work at all. That is considered magic and spellcasting, which is okay if you are trained in Wicca, but is not what this method intends.

Writing a God Letter for a love relationship is very complicated as human beings are involved. I would suggest you practice some other manifestations first.

The Great "What-If"
A True Story

—⟋⟍—

W hat I read in the articles on *www.collapsenet,* indeed in articless posted by media everywhere, is the burning question —What if?

What if our cities and states and countries collapse?

What if we don't have enough time to get our affairs in order before the collapse?

What if we don't have enough food stored?

What if we don't have enough guns to protect us?

What if we don't have enough gold to survive?

What if our loved ones die during the collapse?

What if we die during the collapse?

What if seven billion people die during the collapse?

What if the world goes crazy?

What if the money and power people and bankers take over the world?

What if there is a New World Order?

What if we are all enslaved?

What if we don't know how to grow food?

What if people steal our food?

What if we slowly starve?

What if we have to run away and hide?

What if there become bands of marauding bandits, coming to attack us and steal everything we have, and kill us?

What if? What if? What if?

"What if" can be the voice of a cunning monster—anxiety. That monster can derail our best intentions. Make us turn against people we know, bully those we love. Interfere with our sleep. Make us sick. Bend us into irrationality. Force us to live in a world that doesn't even exist yet— if at all. A world of our minds.

To practice, anticipate, even rehearse scenarios of collapse in order to be prepared, is reasonable.

To live in the shadow of anxiety day after day can actually bring about what one fears.

Anxiety can become a self-fulfilling prophecy.

I once knew a man who created an entire reality with his anxiety. Back in the sixties, he was lonely, sad, paranoid, trapped in his own thoughts. I'll call him Peter. My first husband worked with Peter.

Peter wasn't very old, maybe in his late twenties when I knew him. He had achieved a black belt in karate. I don't know what level of black belt, but pretty high. He participated in karate tournaments and only those few with an equal level black belt could spar with him.

My husband was enthralled and asked Peter to give him karate lessons. Peter was only too happy to oblige, since he loved karate. My husband didn't pay him much money, so I included a home-cooked dinner for Peter once a week after each lesson.

Although Peter was my husband's teacher, I was touched by his sadness and became his friend. I encouraged him to open up and tell me how his life was going.

He told us that wherever he went, out of the blue, guys would pick fights with him. Peter could be walking down a street, minding his own business, and boom! There would be a menace facing him. A man might follow him. A person would cross the street to threaten him. Peter could best all these attackers, because of his karate expertise. Peter proudly explained to my husband that he would teach him how to counterattack these kinds of threats, just as he himself had learned.

I was puzzled. Why was Peter a walking target?

We became acquainted with Peter, and he told us anguished stories of his earlier life. His mother had abandoned him when he was very little. When he was around nine, his father had a heart attack in front of him. The father fell to the ground, hitting his head on the edge of a table as he did so. Peter's father bled to death. There were no relatives to care for Peter, so the court assigned him to foster care. Peter moved from one foster home to another until he was eighteen, six in all, I think he said.

Unfortunately Peter had a problem with his ankles. He wore braces and special shoes for years to strengthen his ankles. This made him a target with the neighborhood and school bullies, who taunted and tormented him, often beating him.

Then Peter discovered karate, and began lessons. He was able to eventually protect himself from bullies. By the time he was around twenty-four he had attained black belt status. His ankles had become strong and he had no further need of braces and shoes. But one disability stayed with Peter. He anxiously believed that the world was out to get him. "What if" a bad guy was waiting for him around that next corner?

When I understood his background, his current life made sense to me.

"Do you think you draw violence to yourself?" I asked him gently.

"It's not my fault. I don't ask for it," Peter hanging his head in despair. "But it is really tiring to always have to watch my back," he added anxiously.

"Maybe fear of the world brings violence to you. Like you're a magnet drawing the attacker. What if you changed the way you think about the world? The world might change."

"I dunno," Peter replied. "I never thought about it." He didn't seem convinced.

"Would you be willing to try?"

"Yeah. Sure. Can't hurt."

"No, it can't," I agreed.

So began an experiment, one I had never been part of before in my life. Neither had Peter.

Peter reported that he practiced changing his thoughts whenever he was out in public. Sometimes saying things out loud when he walked, like, "I'm safe wherever I go." "The world is a safe place." "I don't have to protect myself anymore."

After a few weeks, Peter came to our house one night, breathless with excitement, his face glowing with happiness. He sat down at our kitchen table and told us a story, a new story.

"I was coming out of 7/11, walking to my car. I looked up and saw a guy with scars on his face, glaring at me. I know that look really well. It means trouble. I got ready for him to attack. I kept saying those thoughts, but I didn't think it would work."

I nodded my head.

"Then all of a sudden, the guy seemed to change his mind. He looked away, got into his own car and drove off. That's it."

I hugged him enthusiastically. "You did it!" I exclaimed. "You changed your world."

Although I knew Peter for another few years, he was never again attacked by anyone. He found a wonderful woman to marry. Started a good job out in the desert, where the couple bought a small ranch, with horses and goats and a dog. Peter opened a karate studio out there, his dream. The last time I saw him, Peter was happy. And his world was peaceful.

What if our world is simply a reflection of our anxious and other negative thoughts, attitudes, and emotions?

What if we can change our minds and thus change our world?

What if our world can be harmonious, healthy, and peaceful because of us?

What if all we have to do is get out of our own way? Not *do* something, but *to cease doing* or thinking in inharmonious ways. Or better yet, to think loving thoughts, feel peaceful feelings, "become what we want to see in the world," as Gandhi said. How would we do that?

According to scientific experiments in permaculture, nature wants to come together in harmonious units. When a number of dissimilar life forms are brought together, they eventually attain peace and harmony as one communal unit.

Princeton physicist and Einstein colleague David Bohm came up with two interlinking theories. First, he theorized that subtle levels of reality exist, from which our physical world originates. Secondly, he observed that individual particles in a plasma state behaved less like individuals and more as if they were "connected to one another as part of a greater existence." as author Gregg Braden explains in his book, *The Divine Matrix*.

In other words, everything is connected to everything.

"All things are connected," explained Native American Chief Seattle, long before David Bohm created his theory.

What if all of us seemingly separate individuals are inextricably connected in one gigantic, cosmic way of life?

"All matter originates and exists only by virtue of a force...We must assume behind this force the existence of a conscious and intelligent Mind. This Mind is the matrix of all matter,"—*1944, Max Planck, the father of quantum theory.*

"The...Matrix is our world. It is also everything in our world. It is us and all that we love, hate, create, and experience...we are the canvas, as well as the images upon the canvas. We are the paints, as well as the brushes." —*The Divine Matrix*, Gregg Braden

What if we decide to paint with more harmonious colors? More gentle hues and shades of being? What if we decide to paint harmony now instead of anxiously waiting for some doomsday moment?

When I owned my permaculture farm in Washington, I studied *Gaia's Garden, A Guide to Homescale Permaculture* by Jim Drake and Stuart Pimm, which discussed experiments studying how communities of various and differing organisms form.

I've seen countless times how various plants, trees, and bushes I planted together on my permaculture farm eventually worked together as a unified whole, all members coming together, creating health and well-being for all, and becoming stronger because of their assemblage

What if we humans could be like that? Coming together, to form harmonious groups and tribes? We don't have to wait for a calamity. We have the internet. We could start now. We could "permaculture" ourselves into strong, harmonious, coherent communities, starting with family, friends, and neighbors. Who knows what wonderful things could happen then?

What if we think, feel, and believe that we exist in a healthy, peaceful, loving, joyful world of plenty? Would our world reflect those beliefs back to us? How many people would it take to begin the shift to this ideal loving planet? According to scientific experiments conducted in the 1970s, the square root of one percent of the Earth's population (only 8,000 people) is all that are needed to begin the consciousness shift, more are needed to accelerate the shift, and more to anchor the changes permanently. If that's the case, then it's doable.

What if we are like those particles of plasma or the microbes in tanks of nutrient broth, able to connect in harmonious groups?

What if......

2012, Ascension, Sacred Mayan Calendar, Crop Circles, and Other Cosmic Dances

—ᗰ—

I was listening to a man on YouTube who calls himself Free Spirit. He was passing on an urgent message I have heard a lot in the last several years. The message is that the planet is facing critical and extreme woes in the Third Dimension. That includes accidents such as the Deepwater Horizon oil spill, Fukishima nuclear accident, as well as pollution of air, water, and food, economic meltdowns, political and financial foul-play, and increasing solar, earthquake, and volcanic activity.

Free Spirit, along with many famous and ordinary people, believes our planet Earth is getting ready to ascend to a higher dimension, most likely in 2012. If all this is true, then we, as inhabitants on this planet are faced with choices, whether we are aware of them or not. We can be overtaken by the death of our three-dimensional bodies. Or we can decide to align with the ascension of our planet.

I have been watching the increasing problems with interest. I observed that human beings seem to ignore complications until extreme problems are about to happen. We are not to blame. Our human brains are wired to take action if a "bear is at the cave door" (fight or flight) but longer-lasting, complex worries are tough to get our heads around. Not to mention any disinformation or outright lies perpetrated by media and political sources, for money-and-power advantages.

I'm not blaming anyone about anything, not even the so-called Elite. Being on this planet is a tough job; overwhelming, painful, fear-based, and confusing. Those Elite, with perhaps aggressive or addictive tendencies, tend to get caught up in the game of gain. The rest of us who are simply muddling along do just that…muddle, working hard to keep our family and ourselves above water. Then there are the millions or billions of humans who are either barely surviving on a $1 a day or not surviving at all.

But you know all that. I'm not telling you anything new and different.

In my intense research of several years on all these subjects, I have come to one easy conclusion: There's nothing to worry about.

I have several reasons why I came to my conclusion. The first happened Christmas night 2010. I'm not a Christian (although highly spiritual) so Christmas is not an especially important day on my calendar. However, for other people it is important, so I send presents and greeting cards and pay attention. That night in 2010 I was watching a movie, and then went into the bathroom for a moment. While there I had an experience that changed my life, again. (I've had a few of them.) I felt as though a invisible hand reached into my heart and removed all the fear that was there.

As background, I had become a political activist in 2002, in the lead-up to the Iraqi occupation. I began to quickly and extensively learn about many unpleasant and devious events and decisions seemingly orchestrated by what I called the "money and power people." I became quite fearful, angry, and depressed about what I learned. And helpless. What could I do as one person? In 2004 when I read about peak oil and impending economic crises, I told Paul, my partner, we needed to buy a survival farm for ourselves and our family. I was "informed" by my Council of Elders we had a six-month window to sell our three tiny rentals in California and find a farm.

We ended up on lush acreage on Whidbey Island, Washington, just as the six-month window closed. Then suddenly prices in California plummeted and prices on Whidbey skyrocketed. We were just in time.

Farming was incredibly hard, as we started our permaculture, organic farm from scratch— it had been pastureland for twenty-five years. Paul was elderly and I'm sickly, so it wasn't the smartest decision I've made. But I felt we had no choice. Over the eight years we were there, each of our family members announced they would not move to our farm, not even in an emergency. Okay. So what were we doing this for? I continued to be upset with the state of the world and stored food and other items for the coming catastrophe. Maybe our families would change their minds.

I wrote articles for *Collapsenet.com* (based on Michael Ruppert's movie and book of the same title) on farming tips, and how/what to store. When members on his website started talking about buying guns and ammunition, my soul went on "pause." I wouldn't hurt or kill anyone who wanted food or shelter, so that was out of the question. I decided that whoever might show up in an emergency could share whatever we had. I would show them how to grow food— or—they could kill us. I made my peace with any possible scenario. Then someone asked what I would do if hundreds or thousands of people showed up at our farm after an economic meltdown. What then? I realized that our little two-and-a-half-acre farm was not the solution I had been looking for.

The "removing fear from my heart" episode occurred a few months later and I became quite peaceful. I didn't worry about any planetary, economic, or environmental crisis any more. That's when my researching went into overdrive about higher solutions. I read a book a day for months, to see what other people were doing and saying. I worked with the Oneness Blessing for a while. I had a few episodes of awakening into higher consciousness on a level I had never experienced before. Awakening was like living in a heavenly existence. Although I knew dreadful things were taking place on earth, my fear was gone. But what about our farm?

One day the Oneness Blessing group had an internet hour, which I listened to at a friend's house. The primary gift I got was learning about Carl Johan Calleman and his fascinating book, *The Mayan Calendar and the Transfromation of Consciousness.* He had researched the Mayans for decades as well as had traveled to Mayan territory, learning directly from the Mayan Elders. The book was intensely detailed and it took me twice reading it through to comprehend it. Once I did, I was elated.

This was not the Mayan calendar of 2012 fame. Calleman describes their calendar, not merely of time, but as delineating the evolution of consciousness. The Mayans' calendar described nine creation cycles, each subsequent cycle twenty times shorter than the one before. The first creation cycle started with the big bang; a 15 to 16 billion year cycle which created multi-celled organisms. The next 850 million year cycle created the first animals, and so on. The last cycle, starting February 11 (or March 9), 2011, a cycle of 260 days, fashioned co-creation of consciousness.

All nine creation cycles culminated on October 28, 2011. At that point, the evolution that was planned for Earth had come to fruition.

According to the Mayan calendar as I understand it, no fear is required. We humans are on the exact right path we have always been destined for and designed to travel, from the first moment of the big bang until now. And furthermore, the universe must be sending us the energies and understanding that are needed for this time.

Suddenly, without warning, the Council sent me an urgent message: "Sell the farm. Now!"

I went on the Library internet, sent about fifty messages that we were selling our farm, with a full description. I also immediately wrote a "God Letter," as I wrote about in the chapter, "How to Easily Get What You Want."

The next day a couple showed up and offered us full purchase price for our farm. They had been looking for a farm for five years. (When my email got to a friend, the friend emailed this couple.) Done! End of story. Escrow passed uneventfully. We bought a small house in Port Townsend and settled down. We had a small yard that barely needs tending, a relief after our farm.

What's the point, you may ask, of this long-ish story? It's because I want you to know how the universe works and how it informs us what we need to do at every step on our path through life. We only need to listen (read the chapter entitled "Psychic/Spiritual Discernment"). Also I want to help you understand how I got to this fearless place I now inhabit.

I began researching again, reading a book a day. I worked with Divine Openings for a while. (This is described in the chapter, "The Complete Idiot's Guide to Enlightenment.") I received more insight and more awakenings. Yet something quite unusual was happening to/with me. I began to emotionally and sometimes physically detach from friends, family, life, my body, my home, everything. Also during this time my past displayed itself to me as I forgave, loved, and was grateful to all participants in my life. I told Paul "I feel like I'm dying. Isn't this what people do when they're getting ready to die?"

Whenever I read news items, I periodically asked the Council, "Should I store food or do anything to prepare for disaster?"

"No," they replied. "You're fine."

Then the main spokesperson in my Council of Elders changed. Babaji, who had worked with me for over 40 years, took a backseat while Metatron took over. I like Metatron a lot, because he's quite chatty! And he explains an amazing amount of information to me. He thanked me for my work on this planet. Wow! No one (especially on that level) had ever thanked me before.

I got a new laptop and went on the internet. (I hadn't had internet during the eight years of farming, because we were out in the country, and couldn't get service except via satellite, which was very expensive.) Suddenly my brain exploded with new information. Crop circles, I learned, were ever-expanding in exquisite detail, communicating to us on elevated levels. I learned that Light Energy was coming to us from the Galactic Center, the Photon belt, and from the Virgo constellation, which was changing our DNA, helping our consciousness ascend, and lightening our bodies.

The Elders are probably right. We are fine. There is nothing we need to do.

Drunvalo Melchizedek concluded the same thing. According to him, we have three options:

—The planet continues on as usual. We live and we die and return to the spirit realm, as we always do after physical death.

—At some point the physical Earth goes away and ascends into another dimension. Consequently, our bodies die and we return to the spirit realm.

—We surrender to Source and ascend into the next dimension along with our planet.

Regardless of our choice or how events progress, we win. No problem. We're fine.

Universal Wisdom

—ᴍ—

I have spent much of my adult life studying and practicing spiritual ideals, what I call Universal Wisdom (a phrase from my book, *The Lemurian Way*). These concepts include, but are not limited to, unconditional love, forgiveness, gratitude, mutual respect, surrender, and acceptance. I'm far from any ideal myself, but every time I forget, I pick myself up and continue to practice and hold these concepts close to me.

I came to these views as a result of my life and a desire to heal my misery.

Here's my story, but there is no blame attached: I was molested for years by my father beginning when I was still an infant, then my uncle molested me when I was four. My mother, a closet alcoholic, hated being a woman and a mother, and took it out on me, being angry one minute and abandoning me the next. I was frightened, depressed, confused, and lonely. Early on I became psychic and could hear my spirit guides, the only protection and kindness I had. My antennae became acutely tuned to protect me. I was a sickly child, growing worse as an adolescent, then physically collapsing into chronic fatigue and fibromyalgia after the birth of my second child when I was twenty-seven, often bedridden, in pain, and unable to be gainfully employed. I managed to accomplish a lot within small windows of time and energy, but I've had oodles of downtime to ponder, meditate, and contemplate the universe and my place in it.

Primarily I practiced healing myself of anger, depression, and blame towards those so-called perpetrators by learning and practicing Universal Wisdom. I forgave those who hurt me and then went one step further, and became grateful for my abusers. I did this for my own benefit, so that I could live my life in peace, to alleviate my inner torment.

After the horror of 9/11, I questioned my faith and everything I had learned up to then, and plummeted again into despair and anger. In January 2003 I became a political activist and began to study and learn what the government and the money/control people were up to. Mike Ruppert was part of my curriculum. Everything he said, the books he recommended (which I devoured along with his videos), seemed to be right on the money, so to speak. Not a pretty picture, but I've always been an advocate for clarity and truth. So I was ripe for the next step in his (and my) evolution—collapse: the book, the movie, and the website.

Although I had already been preparing for years, buying a permaculture survival farm, growing fruits and vegetables, storing food and other necessities, I found myself often riding the fear/anger/depression/despair merry-go-round. Up until recently. My son and I have long discussions by phone. I found myself gradually reverting back to pre-9/11 concepts that had brought me peace: Universal Wisdom. I became calmer, stopped yelling at the TV, got off my ranting soapbox, and practiced more fully the quality of life I wanted to live.

As Gandhi said, "Become the change you want to see in the world."

Then came a call for writers on Mike Ruppert's *Collapsenet.com*. Being a published writer and poet, lecturer and teacher, I debated, then sent an article and was accepted. I've written more articles and noticed a funny thing happening. The articles I wrote were upbeat, sometimes humorous, with a positive, spiritual note. I had attained acceptance within myself in the face of collapse! I have moments where I lapse into negative thinking, but I find it easier and easier to return to a tranquil and happy state of mind.

There are several concepts I want to share with you that I have adopted. In this tumultuous time, these concepts are helpful, calming, nurturing, and strengthening, even life transforming.

First is something my spiritual guides ingrained into me: "Everything is perfect, no matter what it looks like, for the purpose of learning, growth and evolution." What??

That means I can't possibly know what consciousness or the Universe has in store for me, or for us humans or the planet itself. But whatever the Universe or higher consciousness is up to, it is for me to learn, grow, and evolve within it. The framework for growth (circumstance) is what is implied as "perfection." So my childhood and three marriages were perfect. My life, although it may not look like it, was perfect. I grew and learned a lot. I became stronger and had more faith in myself. I became compassionate. I learned that I was taken care of when I most needed care. I evolved into a spiritual warrior, a warrior with a heart. Thus, I would not change anything from my past, not one blessed thing.

Prior to learning Universal Wisdom, I might have danced on my parents' graves, thumbing my nose at them. But when my mother died some years ago, I had already forgiven her and was at peace at her passing. I was able to lovingly care for an ailing father for a short time until he died, even praying that he would be spared pain from the cancer—which he was—and he passed quietly.

This brings me to my next point. My spirit guides tell me that in the universe, "everything is connected to everything." I am connected to the planet, water, trees, to other people, birds, insects, rocks, etc. They told me to imagine a giant spider web of existence. Whatever I (or anyone) did to vibrate the spider web could be felt by everyone and everything. In other words, each person can make a difference.

Rupert Sheldrake in his book, *Morphic Resonance,* explains further that

"…energy fields of form evolve and reinforce each other." He discusses some of his experiments with humans, birds, and animals. He concluded that there seems to be a "morphic" field of energy around each living being. This morphic field interconnects and interacts with other fields of energy. What he discovered is that when one morphic field (human, bird, or animal) learns something, that knowledge is passed on to other fields without the need for teaching or observation, through the "spider web of existence."

This phenomenon seems to be especially true with inventions. Often inventors or scientists all over the globe will simultaneously be working on a similar invention or breakthrough. The first person to the patent office is proclaimed the official discoverer.

Another example of this is the "hundredth monkey" syndrome. A number of Japanese scientists were stationed on various small Pacific islands, to observe the effects of nuclear radiation on the wildlife there, primarily monkeys. The scientists were connected via radio, to report their findings to one another. In order to study the monkeys at close range, they dropped sweet potatoes on the beach and then observed the monkeys' behavior. One day a young female monkey took her sweet potato to the ocean and washed off the sand and ate it. During the next few days other monkeys on that island watched her and followed suit. On the day that the hundreth monkey on that island washed off a sweet potato, simultaneously, on ALL the other islands, ALL the monkeys began washing their sweet potatoes in the ocean! Learning is thereby connected to all beings simultaneously. Surely we are as smart as monkeys. Einstein observed this phenomenon of connectedness and called it "spooky action at a distance."

I can influence, either negatively or positively, by how I feel, think, and act. Each person can influence change for the better or worse (via the collective consciousness of the planet).

The good news is that we can make changes by changing ourselves. Back to Gandhi again. Perhaps within ourselves resides a primal place where we can call on spiritual power to make positive changes. If I moan about problems in the world, it is up to me to "change my ways," as Michael Jackson sang in "The Man in the Mirror."

Gregg Braden, who has researched human consciousness for twenty-five years, clarified this phenomenon in a workshop I attended. He explained that scientists now believe that we live in a holographic universe. Gregg showed the audience a picture of a hologram. Then he showed us a minute section of the hologram, in which the piece appeared to be a mirror image of the entire hologram. Then he made a miniscule change in the piece. The entire hologram shifted to become the new image of the small piece. One change makes a difference in the whole.

I have a theory that reflects that idea, based on my observations over the last forty years, which I call Lauren's Laws. "As I transform myself, other people transform themselves in my presence." Similar is the saying, "As above, so below." The microcosm is a reflection of the macrocosm.

In *Loving What Is*, Byron Katie asks four simple questions of each upsetting thought, starting with "Is it true?" then turns the thought upside down, shifting attitudes, changing feelings and behavior. My spirit guides would concur with Katie's premises: everything is perfect, no matter what it LOOKS like.

Scientists have discovered that human emotions affect the magnetic field of our planet. Negative emotions weaken it, while positive (Universal Wisdom) emotions like love, peace, and compassion strengthen it. Earth's magnetic field protects us from solar energy coming from the sun. Too little protection from the magnetosphere can lead to climate change, polar ice melt, even adversely affect human activity. Through HeartMath and the Global Coherence Initiative, tens of thousands of people gather daily to attune their heart energy, sending love and compassion to areas of earthquakes, volcanic eruptions, tsunamis, and war, thereby strengthening the Earth's magnetic field.

I can cry and wail, get angry and depressed for what "they" are doing to our world, or I can courageously change the world, beginning with myself. To become the best me I can be, loving, supportive, compassionate.

I notice that often human beings tend to avoid taking action unless it is absolutely necessary. Perhaps human consciousness is being pushed to the wall, to enable us see what destructiveness we are collectively capable of and participating in. And then to present each of us with the opportunity to make new and better decisions.

Perhaps Consciousness itself is trying to evolve. Perhaps if we join together, we can make a difference, we can change our world into one that is peaceful, harmonious, and healthy.

My spirit guides and Gandhi, Gregg Braden, the Global Coherence Initiative, Rupert Sheldrake, Byron Katie, and others may be wrong. The worst thing that could result in being wrong is that by practicing Universal Wisdom, I will be peaceful and happy, and view the world with courage, willingness, acceptance, love, and even joy.

Are You a Conduit?

—⁓—

Out of seven billion people, there are approximately five million human beings on this planet right now who are Conduits. There is one Conduit for every 144,000 people—men, women, children, babies, old people, disabled people, dying people, those in comas—in every corner of the globe. When a human being dies or is born, there is an instant restructuring, so that every person remains shielded and serviced by a Conduit.

My Council of Elders first explained about Conduits around 1995, and told me that I was a Conduit. I believed them, yet was skeptical at the same time. I needed, wanted proof. So far I have discovered no proof, except what I experience in my own body.

I'll start with some definitions of the meaning of conduit from *Merriam Webster's Collegiate Dictionary*

1) a natural or artificial channel through which something is conveyed
2) fountain
3) a pipe, tube or tile for protecting electric wires or cables
4) a means of transmitting or distributing (such as payments or information)

The Elders extend their explanation into two further classifications. A Conduit is a transformer (converter) and a transponder (a radar set which is tuned to a specific signal).

To Conduct: Act of leading from a position of command; escort; guide. To act as a medium. To show the way.

Conductor: Capable of transmitting a form of energy.

Specifically, the Elders explained that each Conduit receives negative physical, mental and/or emotional energy from their own group of 144,000 individuals, then subsequently cleanses, filters, and neutralizes that energy. The energy next goes deep into the Earth's crystalline iron core, where it is transformed into positive energy, ultimately returning to the surface of the planet, to be utilized by Earth's inhabitants. Why not just send positive energy instead? They haven't explained that to me.

The means of cleansing, filtering, and neutralizing must be done through a physical body. A Conduit requires a three-dimensional body. Therefore, the job of Conduit cannot be done by Ascended Masters, Angels, or ETs—only by ordinary, earthly human beings alive today.

A Conduit agrees to perform this job, and signs the contract, before conception. The job lasts continuously from birth until the last moment of life. A Conduit is a vitally important job for this planet. Without Conduits, I'm told, the Earth would implode with negativity. You know how much negativity currently exists, even with the ongoing help of Conduits. Imagine what existence would be like without Conduits.

Speaking from my own experience, the job of Conduit is difficult, taxing, painful, and emotionally and physically draining. I often feel what the consciousness of the planet is experiencing. I chose to be a Conduit because I have an immense love of our planet, all the people, plants, and animals that exist upon it, and wanted to make a tangible difference. I often regret my agreement, because quite frankly, it makes me sick. I've been sick my entire life and the problems are only getting more intense.

You may be saying to yourself right now: "She must be an idiot to have taken on this job."

I would agree with you. I don't think I realized just HOW difficult and painful it would be to do this job. After all, I agreed to it while still in the spirit realm, without a body or emotions. At the moment of my birth, unpleasant sensations flooded through me and have been doing so ever since. Why am I sick? I think I'm sick so I can remain quiet and conduct energy more efficiently.

So being a Conduit does NOT make me feel special and I don't feel egotistical. (Here! You do it!)

Furthermore, with the culmination of the Mayan calendar of evolution, the energy is increasing exponentially, daily. In the last few months, my circadian rhythm is reversed; I'm up all night and sleep during the day. I also seem to sleep a lot. The Elders told me that both are to protect me from the ever-increasing energies.

The Elders tell me my job will get harder throughout 2012. For example, today is May 1, 2012 and there are Occupy Movements, protests, and events happening globally. I am sicker than usual and woke up feeling really, really ANGRY! And hostile, and irritable, and cranky, and ranting. There's nothing going on in my personal life. I must be absorbing anger from the planet (and my 144,000 dear people).

So I need to relax, do whatever I can to be at peace. Sit back, relax, and let the energies run through me. I don't have to know, nor do I consciously know, how to cleanse and filter. That happens automatically. Thank goodness, or I might make a mess of it!

I 've come to know four Conduits because of publishing this article previously. I am putting out this message to find more of you who are doing the same Conduit job I am. We can become a Conduit Country Club, a Conduit Network, or Conduit Union. We can share our experiences with each other. We can remind each other that we're not crazy or hypochondriacs or lazy bums. Rather we are doing a service to our planet. Indeed, it is at this very crucial time that being a Conduit is of extreme importance.

For those of you who are NOT Conduits, let me tell you some secrets about your feelings:

1. It isn't necessarily your negativity—rather it's your withholding of or denying your emotions—that are difficult for us to process. So feel your feelings all the way to the end. You'll know when you've hit the end, because suddenly you won't be feeling that feeling any more. It could take moments, days or longer to get to the end, but persist.

2. The next worst thing is when you don't let go of the emotion you are feeling. Relax and let the feeling run through you, as if it is water, without stopping it or holding on. Feelings and emotions are just vibratory energy, although they seem very real.

3. And the third worst thing is when you inflict your emotions on others—particularly anger, hate, and vengeance, which are the building blocks of conflict of all kinds (internal, familial, and global); war; disease; and sometimes Earth changes. You can process your emotions within yourself without abusing others. If need be, go for a walk in the woods (or a drive your car to a deserted mall) and scream. Hit a pillow. Cry. See a counselor. Talk to a trusted friend. Whatever it takes.

But…aren't negative emotions bad? Nope. In fact, emotions are what we are here to learn about and evolve THROUGH.

Negative behavior—what you do to yourself or another goes out into the universe like a sledgehammer (like greed and other negative behavior). Remember that, when you are treating yourself or someone else badly.

Negative thoughts, too, have consequences. Just ask me, and the other Conduits, and we'll tell you! So when you have a negative thought, all you have to do is briefly notice it, then ignore it. The thought isn't real. It will disappear. If it doesn't leave, you can always read the chapter, "The Complete Idiot's Guide to Enlightenment" and apply the necessary actions to your thoughts.

The next time you suppress, hold onto, inflict your emotions on others, or behave or think negatively, remember me and the other five million Conduits trying to make life better. We will do our jobs anyway. But we could use a little help from you. Thanks!

One more thing—because of the changes that are happening to humankind at this point in evolution, we are ALL beginning to experience each other's emotions, behaviors, and thoughts. You will experience those as your own, if you haven't already. We are all connected as one and are beginning to wake up to that connection. Negativity hurts us all.

For those of you who ARE Conduits, the universe appreciates you and your work. I know this job can be thankless sometimes. I know you can feel inundated by stuff that isn't even yours. But keep up the good work. I believe we are coming to the end of the need for our job. Perhaps also the Conduit goes both ways. Maybe we conduct energy, knowledge, and wisdom to and from others. We receive as well as give. I like that idea.

If all Conduits are similar to the four I know personally, one may:
1) Have a very strong body (although ill);
2) Had a trauma or two early in life (which makes one strong and opens one's channels);
3) Be connected to Ascended Masters, Angels, Archangels, or some Higher spirit that one is aware of;
4) Be highly sensitive to others and the planet.

Are you a conduit?

Everything is Perfect, No Matter What it Looks Like

—ⷶⷶⷶ—

This is a mantra my Council of Elders has been repeating to me for decades. It hasn't always been easy for me to understand. Or to accept. But when I do accept that everything is perfect, I feel better, at peace.

Perfect doesn't mean like "perfect health" or "perfect happiness" or perfect like faultless, flawless, or unspoiled. Perfect in Elder-Speak means simply acceptance of the way things are.

I suffered—physically, emotionally, mentally, financially, and sexually—for years. No one could say that all those years have been "Perfect" from a textbook definition. But because I came into my life to heal and balance old relationships, to atone for old patterns of behavior from past lives, as well as to get to a point where I didn't need to reincarnate any more, then I could say my life has been perfect. All my difficulties have compelled, forced, and led me to look inside, to find out how to make myself feel better. My feeling better has come from learning to love, accept, forgive, and be grateful to everyone and everything, including my body.

Yesterday I "met" a wonderful woman through Facebook, a healer and a clairvoyant, who was moved to help me feel better. She told me she would do healing on me during the night and today I would feel so much better, less pain, more relaxation. I don't. I feel tremendously worse, more pain, disturbed sleep, even dreaming about feeling bad.

I forgot. I forgot all of the healers, and Reiki masters, and doctors, Naturopaths, specialists, and chiropractors, masseurs, physical therapists, counselors, therapists, nutritionists, allergists, acupuncturists, and workshop leaders that I have gone to during four decades who could not "heal" me— plus I often ended up feeling much worse. It wasn't that I couldn't accept healing. It was because I was "fine" the way I was, the way I was set up to be, the way I am supposed to be in order to heal my life from a higher, spiritual perspective.

The Elders tell me that everything is perfect because we are here to learn, grow, and evolve. Since the Higher Source is in everything and is everywhere and has set up our planet and our lives to be exactly what they are, there is nothing wrong, nothing that needs to be fixed. All lessons, including political, financial, social, and environmental "wrongs" are meant to stimulate us into learning. Learning what? Each of us is here to learn our own perfect lessons. You may be physically healthy, but need to learn something different than me. I couldn't say. I don't know. But I assume our learning includes Universal Wisdom—such as love, surrender, trust, gratitude, compassion, and forgiveness.

Furthermore, I am a Conduit. That means I work 24/7 at a job that filters, cleanses and neutralizes "negativity" from 144,000 individuals— through my physical body. My body needs to be a certain way in order to fulfill that job. Also, what my body is experiencing may not even be my stuff at all.

Do I like suffering and pain? No, not really. I'm not saying that my life is easy. Far from it. I can sometimes be heard complaining or crying to my Elders to help me, to stop the pain, ease my suffering. Their response is usually, "Just relax Lauren. You're fine." Once I relax, accept, and surrender, I do feel better, amazingly enough. Then I can continue to work on my gratitude and forgiveness of my body and the situation.

In my early twenties, I was a participant in a few miraculous healings of other people. When I found out about a problem, I would yell (yes, yell) at the Universe and demand help from Mother/Father god, Jesus Christ, all the healing angels and anyone else who could help, to save an individual. Then I was "told" what to do. After following the directions, a miracle would transpire. I'm convinced these miracles were part of the individual's learning process—apparently, or I don't think they would have healed.

One was a fifteen-year-old girl who had been hit by a car and developed gangrene on her upper thigh. Her doctors decided they would amputate the leg at the hip. Her leg was saved at the last minute. The gangrene had disappeared the morning of the surgery.

Another was my father, who had a cancerous tumor the size of a golf ball in his stomach. When he got to the hospital for more tests and surgery to cut it out, the tumor had disappeared. He was released, without surgery, and lived another twenty-five years.

The third was a young single mother of twins. She had Type I Diabetes her whole life. Her retinas were detaching and she was going blind quite rapidly. After I asked for help from the Higher Realm, her retinas reattached. This was to the amazement of her eye specialist, who had been doing laser treatment on her with no positive effect. Thirty years later she still has her eyesight and has raised her daughters to adulthood.

However, a fourth time, a friend of mine asked if I could psychically attend a friend's sixteenth surgery, to ask for the same kind of divine help. I agreed. When I arrived at the entrance of the surgical room, a "steel door" closed in my consciousness. "You are not needed here," I was told and I left. The girl died a week later. Everything is perfect, no matter what it looks like. I am not in charge. The Universal Source is in charge, which works in tandem with each individual's course of learning.

I once lectured to a group of Jewish people. I brought up this cosmic decree of everything being perfect.

They were outraged. "What about the holocaust?" they demanded.

I shrugged. "I don't know what the lessons were for any of those millions of people that died," I replied. "Or for all the survivors. Or the Nazis. Or Americans. Or us today. I don't know what each person was to learn or possibly to teach others. All I know is that everything is perfect, no matter what it looks like.

A dear friend of mine, who is a counselor, decided he liked the concept. "So once a person accepts that everything is perfect, then the situation changes!" he exclaimed.

"No," I replied. "Everything is perfect, even if it NEVER changes."

This concept flies in the face of everything that humans want to do—to fix, improve, heal, make better, reorganize. I sometimes wonder if the condition of our environment is due to our over-zealous desire for change—for something "better." I'm not implying that we should never take an action. But it is up to each individual to intuit what that appropriate action might be.

In fact, I have thought long and hard about the current human condition on our planet which seems out of control, with pollution, wars, starvation, greed, financial ruin, and any number of issues to consider. But what if all those things are perfect, in order for all of us humans to learn, grow, and evolve? I don't know. I'm not privy to that information. But it is worth thinking about.

As the Elders repeat the mantra, I relax and continue to learn what I need to learn.

That means that all my friends plus those I disagree with—and the rest of the seven billion people I don't even know—are right.

Battle of Beliefs

—〰—

I sometimes feel like George Carlin who said (I'm paraphrasing), "I don't feel like a member of the human species. I feel connected to protons and atoms, though…"

What is it that makes me feel separate?

When it appears the world is going to "hell in a handbasket," why do people focus on that?

My son Nathan complained to me in a poem:

> *The financial collapse, coming sooner than you think*
> *Don't watch CNN, MSNBC, or Fox, because they all stink*
> *Get out of the cities and buy a farm*
> *A psychotic government intends you harm*
> *First goes the euro, then the dollar*
> *Buy silver and gold, this I must holler*
> *Coming soon, food riots and civil unrest*
> *Will put our Constitution to the test*
> *Or just watch football and Dancing with the Stars*
> *Take your anti-depression pills and fill up the bars*

Thanks for your thoughts, Nate!

On the opposite end of the spectrum, I warn of impending miracles. We can make a change in consciousness. One person can make a difference. Together we can help our beautiful Earth recover, endure, heal. Our species can survive, along with all the other wonderful species we're joined with.

What makes me feel as though I'm "blowin' in the wind" with these ideas, as Bob Dylan sang?

I think it's because the main war on this planet seems to be a Battle of Beliefs:

Christian versus Muslim versus Jew versus Hindu versus Atheist versus Pagan.

Conservative versus Progressive versus Green versus Save-the-Whales versus Save-the-Corporations.

MSNBC versus Fox News versus The Daily Show.

Female versus male.

Young versus old.

Conservation versus Keeping-all-Your-Lights-Burning.

Rich versus Poor.

Name Brand versus Thrift Store.

Organic versus Agri-business.

Us versus Them.

We're having a Tower of Babel convergence of Beliefs—a Bottleneck of Beliefs, a Bombardment of Beliefs, with so many people simultaneously saying so many different things, it's dizzying and confusing. What's true? What's not?

My belief is better than your belief.

My belief is real. Yours isn't.

You must be crazy to believe like that.

You'll go to hell if you believe in that. You'll go to heaven if you believe in this.

You'll be miserable if you believe in that.

You'll be happy if you believe this.

You're doomed if you don't believe this.

I'm the only one (or part of a group) who's right. Everyone else is ignorant, stupid, crazy or burying their head in the sand

The Battle of Beliefs makes ordinary people into enemies. Enemies are dehumanized individuals who are easy to devalue, push to the sidelines, even murder. How do some Americans think of Iraqis and Afghanis? Or Middle Easterners or Muslims? Remember Bosnia and "ethnic cleansing?" How do Israelis think of Palestinians? How about the Rwandan ethnic cleansing, where the Hutus regarded the Tutsis as cockroaches. How difficult is it to squash a cockroach?

But—what if all feelings and thoughts and beliefs are created equal?

What if nobody's wrong?

What if everyone's right?

That would be a relief.

What if each of us lives in our own separate reality? And in this reality, a separate universe that each of us inhabits, everything is true and correct and real.

That means….

I can believe in a horrible collapse of our civilization. And I'm right.

or

I can believe we are creating a wonderful, miraculous shift into a golden age. And I'm still right.

Which reality do I choose to live in? Or do I straddle the fence? Weighing my options? Hedging my bets?

That means that no matter what a person says to me, I can simply reply, "You're right." Is that mind-boggling? Can I do it? Do I need to do it?

That means that:

Mother Theresa was right. Saddam Hussein was right. G.W. Bush was right. Gandhi was right.

That means that all my enemies and all my friends—and all the rest of the seven billion people I don't even know—are right.

That means I don't have to fight over, argue, or debate anything. I don't have to fight my own Battle of Beliefs anymore. I'm not better than you. I'm not better—or worse—than anyone. I am purely, simply, distinctly myself. The same as everyone. Existing in my own wonderful universe, as each person lives in his or hers. Whatever my universe is, I'm right.

That means that peace exists out beyond the field of battle. In the verdant meadow beyond the Battle of Beliefs lies peaceful co-existence. Cooperation. Harmony. Community. Oneness. Absolute equality.

Scientists and quantum physicists have done experiments over the last decade or so and have concluded that "everything is connected to everything." Many ancient religions and spiritual traditions concur. That means that even if I believe I'm separate from everyone, every event, every blessing, every awful tragedy, I'm not. My personal universe is connected invisibly and attached to every other personal universe, whether I want to be or not, whether I like it or not.

That puts a different spin on my world. The "blame game" comes to an end. There is no one to blame for the world's problems: climate change, pollution of water, earth, and air, too many people, too much money and power in the hands of those who are greedy, or economic collapse. "Somebody else will fix those problems," I can say. "It's not my worry."

But—if everything is connected to everything, while I live in my own universe of beliefs, then the only one to hold responsible in my universe—is me. The only one who can fix my universe is me. The only one who can alter my beliefs is me. Changing my beliefs can change my experiences. Changing my beliefs *does* change my experiences. I've tried it, and experienced miracles. Miracles live in a peaceful pasture outside the Battle of Beliefs.

Contemplating Survival

—ɯɯ—

I am a spiritual survival pragmatist. That means that for the last eight years I have been assessing survival scenarios, once I understood peak oil and economic/resource implications. I put myself into a state of mind of "what if" civilization as I knew it collapsed. Where should I go? How could I best prepare? What would I need? What would I have to do? Learn? Practice? My inner voice advised me I had a six month window to accomplish my first step. I trust my inner voice and follow its messages.

The obvious priority was growing, preserving, and storing food. I was fortunate because I had been practicing organic gardening for thirty years. But along with food came questions about security, water availability, population density, cooking, heating, and the consciousness level of the people around us, neighbors and friends.

So where to locate? Southern California, where we lived, was out of the question. Due to climate change, the weather was getting hotter every year, plus it's a desert with a terrible lack of water. Not to mention it's horrendously overpopulated and there was no farming land available for any affordable price.

In 2004 I asked for help from the Universe to direct me. The first internal message I got was to sell everything. We immediately put our little condo up for sale. The second message was that we had a six month window to buy a farm and sell our other properties.

A friend recommended we look into the Pacific Northwest, where there was a rain shadow, a moderate climatic area stretching between two mountain ranges. Paul and I traveled there and started exploring the area. Nothing much interested us. We had a day to ourselves and decided to take a ferry to a nearby island. We immediately fell in love and knew the island was where we wanted to live and survive. We returned to California. Our condo had already sold (this was before the collapse of the housing bubble). We put our other two tiny rentals up for sale. My husband returned to the island to search for a farm. The day he arrived, a property had gone on the market with two-and-a-half acres of abandoned pasture land with a three-bedroom house and outbuildings. The property was priced $40,000 below market, because the seller was getting married and wanted to sell quickly. She did. To us. Once we sold everything, six months almost to the day, the farm was ours, free and clear, no mortgage. Shortly afterwards, housing prices in California fell while housing prices in Washington surged. We had accomplished our goal just in time.

I learned about permaculture from a Peak Oil Conference at Antioch College. We couldn't attend because we were searching for property suitable for a farm, but I listened to audio recordings. The most upbeat person I listened to from the conference was a woman who talked enthusiastically about permaculture. She got my full attention.

While we waited for escrows to close on our condo and the farm, I voraciously absorbed everything I could find on permaculture and studied day and night. When we moved to our survival farm, I wrote to all our friends and relatives and explained the farm's purpose to them. "If anything horrible happens to the economy," I told them, "you can come here. There will be food, water, and shelter." I grin now when I contemplate what would happen if everyone arrived. We'd have to get busy building those small Hobbit-like Habitat Huts I've been reading about!

That first week, although it was a cold February in 2005, we started planting fruit and nut trees, fourteen kinds of berries, currants, grapes, herbs, native plants, whatever we could afford and could get into the ground. I intuited we had no time to lose and had to get trees and shrubs growing and producing as fast as possible. Who knew how much time we had?

As I realize now how perfect our farm was, I see miracles everywhere. Listening to internal and external guidance certainly played a vital role.

The soil on our farm was considered some of the best in the area. We had a well, along with newly-installed buckets, barrels, and a cistern to collect water. We had a moderate climate, and got about sixteen inches of rain a year, which translates into about 5,000 gallons of saved water from our roof (our house was 1,400 square feet). We diverted all our household grey water (except for toilets) down to irrigate the land below.

The island was somewhat isolated, with a small and communal populace. The atmosphere was primarily rural with many residents already growing their own food, raising ducks, chickens, turkeys, sheep, goats, llamas, alpacas, cows, etc. We had five thriving farmer's markets and lots of CSA's (Community Sponsored Agriculture). To get to the island meant either taking a ferry or traveling over a suspension bridge. In an extreme economic collapse, the ferries won't run and the bridge could be easily defended (or even blown up to isolate the island from the outside world).

Most people on the island were friendly, helpful, and outgoing. Our farm was situated along the only highway, where people could see our farm, and watch our progress. We had many folks stopping by to inquire just what the heck we were doing. Some became friends. We also taught people about the concepts of permaculture, which include enriching the soil, using chicken tractors, building swales, utilizing grey water and water recycling, worm bins, organic gardening, interplanting and companion planting, mulching, and how nature will fill in the gaps to make lush growth without much irrigation or fertilizing if we planted accordingly. Even though we were permaculture novices, we were written up in local newspapers, asked to lecture locally about what we were doing, and had classes and tour groups stop by to get a quick lesson or two. A home study school came and utilized some of our land to teach their students how to plant food. The class took their proceeds to a local food bank.

I loved it when people brought their garden waste to us to mulch our fledgling plants—and their accompanying children got curious. I often took the kids to see the chickens, had them pet them (our hens were quite friendly), perhaps discovering a freshly-laid still-warm egg, which I gave to each child to take home to cook. I felt as though I was planting seeds of awareness in these young persons.

Many people who had relocated to the island say they felt like they were guided to move here, just like us. It's almost as if a group consciousness had brought us together to a place that was highly suitable for small, sustainable, community, and survival living.

So I say to listen to your inner wisdom, no matter how crazy or illogical it seems. Trust whatever messages you get, from both yourself and other sources, and then follow those messages. It's not too late to start. An organic nurseryman once told me: "The best time to plant a fruit tree was ten years ago. The next best time is now!"

The most important aspect of being a spiritual survival pragmatist is to both give and receive. If I need something, I ask for it. From a friend. In the newspaper. In the local freecycle (you can sign up for freecycle at *Yahoo.com*). If I have surplus, I give it away. In fact, a major principle of permaculture is to "share the abundance." I give to food banks. To needy friends. To a sick neighbor. To give to someone because I just want to. And giving away makes me feel good while it helps another.

Sharing is part of my "Universal Bank Account." When I give something away, that is tallied in my bank account in the form of energy. When I need something, the Universe withdraws it from my bank account and I receive what I need. Usually when I give to an individual or an organization, I do not receive it back directly from the individual or organization. I receive it later in the form I need it.

The universe, and nature, is wildly, exuberantly abundant and generous. Just contemplate the number of seeds in a dandelion or in a carrot that has gone to seed.

I'm a pragmatist, because the Universal Bank Account system has successfully worked for me for over fifty years (including years ago when I was temporarily jobless, homeless, and destitute but miracles kept happening to keep me afloat, give me furniture, find me a job, and send Paul to me).

We needed some ducks on our farm to control the growing slug and snail population. Island folks found out and they gave us thirteen ducks within a week. Goodbye slugs and snails.

I realized we needed a feral cat to reduce the growing rodent population, due to extensive mulching. The day after my realization, three feral cats showed up and have been living and hunting on our farm ever since. Did someone send a cat telegram?

We lacked canning jars to preserve our bounteous harvest. Within a week we were given five boxes of jars, lids, and rings—and an offer of a pressure canner. And the list goes on and on.

A friend of mine, Barb, and I started a service the first fall I lived on Whidbey, when our farm had gone to sleep and I had time on my hands. We called it the Free-For-All. She and I drove around and picked up good, usable items from local thrift stores that they couldn't sell or didn't have room for. Those items would have ended up in the landfill. Then on Saturdays we put those items on tables in my front yard and gave it all away. Every week we got more and more merchandise, clothing, and bigger items and furniture. The Free-For-All grew so large, we ran out of room to store stuff in our house and garage during the week. We gave all of it away on Saturdays except for a few broken items. We saved it from the landfill. People received items they needed or wanted. We saved money for the thrift stores, who had to pay to dispose of stuff. (They cut their dump fees in half!) A number of people started volunteering to help us set up and take down. We eventually stopped the Free-For-All out of exhaustion, a lack of storage room, and also because our farm was waking up in the Spring and needed our full attention. But I have never forgotten our adventure.

I think the Free-For-All is a new paradigm, a new consciousness. Or maybe it's a practice our ancestors knew well, but which we have forgotten. We all have excess stuff others need. Others have stuff we need. After sharing, our Universal Bank Account increases and pays big dividends for everyone.

I have read articles on *collapsenet.com* (the first online how-to for Preppers), of people storing food, water, and supplies for their families—with guns to protect their caches. But I chose to go in a different direction. I stored massive amounts of food, seeds, and other items for family, friends, and even people whom I may not yet know. People who may have come to our farm, starving, desperate, scared. I planned to invite them to dinner and to stay. To teach them how to grow food for their futures, and teach them to become part of our extended family on the farm, of the human family.

I'm not arbitrarily selfless. I'm not a martyr. I just know how the universe works.

Perhaps selfishness and greed is what has gotten humankind into the predicament we find ourselves in today. Perhaps it is time to change the paradigm, change our consciousness, one person at a time. Perhaps that is the silver lining in the ominous cloud of economic problems we see looming.

Am I a Pollyanna? No, I don't think so. Remember, I'm a pragmatist. I only practice things with which I have experimented that work.

Do my stories make sense in the light of a possible collapse or emergency? I think they do. We will be neighbors together in a catastrophe. But collapse doesn't just portend survival of the fittest. We may survive better if we regard each other as friends and not adversaries.

A line I adore from the movie, *The Great Race,* as Tony Curtis explains to Jack Lemmon when they're stranded on an iceberg: "One Wayleeok Indian in a blanket may freeze. But two Wayleeok Indians in a blanket can survive."

How I conduct myself with others may mean the difference between life and death, for all of us, and not just during an emergency. It means rehearsing in present time as well. And so I practice building my Universal Bank Account for an unknowable future, but one in which I anticipate working with others, with whom I will both give and receive.

P.S. I had an abrupt change of heart December 25, 2010 (see the next chapter, "Removing Fear From My Heart"). We sold our farm in 2011 in one day, getting our full asking price, and moved into a wonderful house in Port Townsend. Paul and I loved our time in permaculture farming and were on to our next Big Adventure.

Removing Fear From My Heart

—m—

For decades I was worried, scared, terrified of what, might, could, or would happen in our world. Late Christmas night 2010, I had a vision, an epiphany, an experience which removed the certainty of collapse from my heart, like a giant hand reached inside and removed that fear. I felt spun in a centrifugal vortex of energy, perhaps creating a whole new reality. I suddenly became aware that I can't "feel" collapse of civilization anymore. It doesn't feel true in my body. Since I trust my intuitive body completely, my "truth meter" as I call it, what I received is a clear message that collapse has been replaced. With what? As the character Dave Bowman luminously said in the movie, *2010,* the sequel to *2001: A Space Odyssey,* I feel that what's coming is "something wonderful."

This "something wonderful" feels like truth in every cell of my body. In my heart. I know it to be so, as much as I've known that collapse was true for me for the last seven years, without a shadow of a doubt. Now—in the twinkling of an eye, as they say—events, maybe even time-space, abruptly changed for me. From one paradigm (collapse) to its opposite (something wonderful) in a nanosecond. It's as though I've jumped across a consciousness chasm into a new dimension. I'm happy, joyful, and full of loving feelings. I can hardly believe the enormous shift in me.

How did I change? I'm not sure. But I have a gut feeling that a number of people on our planet have been working overtime, changing our collective consciousness to something much more pleasing than a brutal collapse of our economy, environment, species, etc. (Gregg Braden in *The Divine Matrix* says that the square root of one percent of the world's population is all it takes to change consciousness—approximately 8,000 people.) I know the few weeks before Christmas, as I'd written my articles, the articles (and I) had been getting more positive and upbeat. Usually the period between Thanksgiving and Christmas is traditionally the hardest part of the year for me. I've always been depressed, agitated and lonely. I've hated the holidays for decades. But this year—for the first time—I've felt peaceful, joyful, and happy.

This new reality feels smooth, like gentle ripples on the pond of creation. I'm waxing lyrical because this is very hard to put into words and I'm having fun experiencing it!

Years ago, when I was writing *The Lemurian Way* with my Council of Elders, they kept repeating a phrase that they drummed into me: "Everything is perfect, no matter what it looks like." Now I have a deep experience of what that means, because the future I now contemplate feels sweet and lovely, truly perfect. I can only feel good things for the future.

Bad things that happened in my life I now feel as wonderful; each difficult step, each trauma, each betrayal leading me here, to peace and delicious gratitude. I now believe my part in this new age is to be happy, joyful, peaceful, forgiving, compassionate, and loving—no matter what anything looks like. It is as though the Universe is evolving through me, as me, to a state of consciousness more beautiful, more kind and gentle, than anything I've ever had in my life or even contemplated.

If you think I've gone 'round the bend, a little light in the head, a can short of a six-pack, join the group. If I wasn't having the experience, I would say so too!

String theorists and quantum physicists have been discussing alternative realities for years, anywhere from eleven different dimensions of reality to infinite dimensions and multi-verses. Have I somehow jumped into another dimension? The world looks approximately the same, yet I'm different in it. And people are reacting differently to me. I want to put my arms around each individual and hug him or her. I see each person as a wonderful part of me, connected to me, yet uniquely her or himself.

I've known many pieces of universal wisdom and have practiced for forty years. But I forgot all that after 9/11, the event which traumatized my soul for a decade, made me question everything. I'm coming back to myself, new and improved.

Years ago the Elders asked me go on an excursion to Homeless Park, where homeless people, junkies, alcoholics, prostitutes, and other lost people hung out. I was afraid to go and asked if we could bring Paul along. "Of course." So Paul and I went to Homeless Park together. I had no idea what I was going there to do or learn.

We parked the car. The Guys (as I call the Elders) encouraged us to walk into the park, pick a bench, and sit down. We did so. Not long after that a young woman, maybe early thirites, wandered along and sat down on the bench next to me. She was filthy dirty, her claw-like nails long and broken, her hair stringy and unkempt. She seemed like she was stoned or drunk, definitely not rational, as she muttered to herself. Her face might have once been lovely, but it looked like someone had taken a razor or knife to her face, which was crisscrossed with deep, red scars. She frightened me and I moved to the edge of my seat.

As I sat and listened to her incoherent ramblings, the Guys quietly said to me, "See the face of God in her."

I took a deep breath. I found it difficult to see what they asked and sat for a long time staring at her. "Face of God, face of God," I too was muttering. After a while, my vision slowly shifted, and I was able to see the face of God in her! She was the same woman, but my attitude towards her was different.

I felt peaceful, ecstatic, and deliriously happy. I could feel beams of love shooting out of my heart towards her. After a couple of minutes, the woman got up and wandered away. We were then allowed to leave, the lesson over.

Several days later I was walking down the street to the grocery store. Coming towards me were two young men, dressed like gang members, swaggering along. I felt suddenly frightened, then remembered, "face of God. Oh yeah." I shifted my mental attitude and the young men shifted too. They both came past me, smiling friendly smiles. One of them said to me, "Have a great day!" and they walked on.

I'm used to having unusual experiences, life-changing experiences. Christmas night was yet another step in my evolution.

I can see everyone with the face of God. My parents. Bankers. Politicians. Media. Corporations. Everything is perfect, no matter what it looks like.

What is going on? I feel some kind of a miracle is happening. Some shift of energy or awareness or consciousness is transpiring.

Sounds kooky, doesn't it? Yet I welcome the future, beams of love shooting out of my heart towards it and all the people in it. Face of God. Face of good.

A New Theory of Crop Circles

—m—

Crop Circles are a conscious, well-thought-out-and-executed PLAN by Beings of Higher and Compassionate consciousness designed especially to help us "wake up." Crop circles are a deliberate and purposeful way of pushing us to pay attention, in order to raise our group consciousness into the Fifth Dimension. "They" are forming crop circles, which are meant to accelerate our evolution, in ever-increasing vibrations consisting of:

- Sacred geometry
- Complex mathematical formulas that some musicians say are harmonic octaves of each other
- Binary codes
- Fibonacci designs as in nature
- Sacred Platonic spheres (Plato himself talked about the Music of the Spheres)
- Higher vibrational sounds
- Pictograms and symbols that reverberate in our collective unconscious

- Exquisite, playful, and artful patterns of beauty, symmetry, and perfection.

Furthermore, although being in the presence of a crop circle is often life-altering, being physically present isn't necessary. One can look at an image and it will have the same effect.

How Did I Arrive At That Idea?

1. Research and investigation—As in everything I (as an intense Scorpio) get interested in, I research and study everything on the subject I can find and read voraciously. I've been studying and researching crop circles for over thirteen years. I had stopped my research some time ago, since it seemed all the crop circle experts had come to a dead end. By whom and how are crop circles formed, and for what reason? No one knows. All are in agreement, however, that crop circles require some form of "intelligence" or higher consciousness. (A couple of months ago I got passionately interested in crop circles again, and started watching many documentaries that have been produced lately, going to expert websites and following videos on YouTube.)

2. I feel personally involved. Read on and you'll see what I mean.

To me, the most important unanswered questions about crop circles are:

—What are crop circles for?

—What are the crop circles trying to communicate to/with us?

According to Colin Andrews and other collective researchers, about twenty percent of all crop circles are considered to be authentic—not man-made, natural, or hoaxed. Mathematicians, engineers, astronomers, molecular biologists, musicians, doctors, scientists, computer analysts, and many other experts have helped to create the specifications for authenticity which include:

—Crop circles appear all over the world, in cereal crops, as well as in snow, ice, and sand

—A dozen or more crop circles will often appear the same night

—Absence of human trails leading into or anywhere near a pristine crop circle

—Crop circle designs becoming increasingly more intricate, using geometrical and mathematical formulas that would take a group days to create (not in the few hours or even minutes crop circles appear;

—A number of reliable eye witnesses seeing crop circles "form" within a few seconds—usually accompanied by mysterious golden globes of light

—Crops that are studied inside the circle show a changed molecular and cellular structure compared with those outside a circle

—Stems of a crop can be bent to a ninety degree angle at a nodule without breaking; sometimes the nodule has been burst open, as if heated to an extreme temperature (this cannot be replicated in natural surroundings)

—Stems of crops intricately woven together

—Measured electromagnetic energy is different within the circle than outside

—A distinct sound has been heard and recorded within circles, even by the BBC—sometimes during the interval that a crop circle is being formed

—"Some patterns also displayed exact numerical relationships, all of them involving a diatonic ratio, the simple whole-number ratios that determine a scale of musical notes"

—Electronic devices stop working or break within a circle

—No natural phenomenon explains the incredibly complex, exacting, beautiful patterns that appear

—Modern technology does not yet have the skill required to create a crop circle

—People experience a unique "energy" inside a crop circle, an altered state. Some people get sick; others euphoric; some become meditative, while all are fascinated.

The Most Important Scientific Finding That Triggered My Attention:
Measurements have been taken of people's endocrine system (pituitary, thyroid, adrenal, and pineal glands) inside and outside crop circles. There are distinct alterations in the glandular functioning of human beings inside crop circles!

When I heard about this element of the research, my ears perked up—again for personal reasons.

I have been sick and disabled for over forty years, partly because of glandular dysfunction. I have been to dozens of doctors, alternative health care providers, physical therapists, nutritionists, naturopaths, environmental doctors, herbalists, homoeopathists, as well as Reiki masters and other healers—and failed to get "well."

Additionally I am highly psychic, which is said to come from the pineal gland, considered a means of psychic awareness and communication with the unseen world. My psychic abilities include communication with and teachings from invisible Beings—Ascended Masters and the Archangel Metatron—of a highly spiritual, ethical, and benevolent nature—for years. I can't usually see these Beings, but I can hear and feel them quite easily. They have been instrumental in a number of miracles in my life.

But what does my being both sick and psychic have to do with crop circles, you may ask?

What if my "sickness" is due to almost continuous exposure throughout my lifetime to advanced beings with a highly elevated vibration? What if I'm not actually sick, but vibrating in a different dimension, which then interferes with normal physical, three-dimensional functioning?

Many believe our planet is "ascending" into the fifth dimension. A lot of people report getting sick with differing symptoms, perhaps due to the increased energetic vibrations coming into our bodies and consciousness. I've found lists on the internet describing these symptoms.

The "ascension sickness," then, could be a manifestation of elevating consciousness, with our physical body's reactions, to higher dimensions.

Sacred Sites Contain Features Found At Crop Circles:
Some researchers believe that ancient peoples may have created their sacred sites (like Stonehenge and Avebury) on and over existing crop circles.

To elaborate:

—Visiting sacred sites helps to elevate consciousness. Before becoming housebound I traveled extensively to sacred sites, then returned home, wrote and published articles on them, and created a website (*Time Travel.com*) devoted to sacred sites and companies offering metaphysical tours to those sacred places.

While I haven't visited a crop circle in person, I find the following significant similarities between sacred sites and crop circles:
- Geometric alignment
- Beautiful and harmonious design
- A sense of being in an altered state while at the site
- Being purposefully created for inexplicable reasons
- Lack of modern understanding as to how or why the sacred site was created
- A change in consciousness after a visit
- Crop circles appear most numerous near sacred sites, especially in England

In my opinion, the most spectacular specimens of sacred sites are in Egypt. I believe each Egyptian site, and often various locations within a site, contain its own particular energy, design, appearance, and purpose. A specific being (like Isis, Osiris, Anubis) is said to have a "home" at a specific sacred site.

Each Neter contains its own vibration, energy, and purpose. (e.g., Isis at Philae represents motherly love, wifely devotion, fierce love, healing, etc.) Therefore, sites in Egypt could be deliberately constructed with specific spiritual purposes in mind. I believe the sites were meant to interact with human consciousness, to communicate higher meaning.

Some Examples of Spiritual Purposes In Egyptian Sacred Sites:

—The so-called sarcophagus in the King's Chamber of the Great Pyramid transports individuals who lay in it to an altered place (or dimension), primarily the stars, called The Duat, a highly sacred Place, by the Egyptians.

—People who visit The Pit at the bottom of the Great Pyramid often report unpleasant experiences. The Pit was allegedly used for priestly initiations. Ancient participants would climb down into the Pit, thereby visiting the dark side of their soul, perhaps remembering other lifetimes, and hopefully returning unscathed. Shamanic initiations worldwide include difficult initiatory experiences.

—The most important is in Seti I's Temple at Abydos, where the walls are extensively and beautifully carved. Allegedly initiates traveled there, and were taught the Egyptian Mystery School lessons by simply gazing at the carvings, feeling the energy, whereby "learning" would mysteriously transmit itself into the person's body, molecules, and awareness. This is what I believe is happening at Crop Circles.

Crop circles started appearing with regularity in the 1970s. The first ones were fairly simple; circles, or circles within circles. Then as human beings found themselves increasingly drawn by the thousands to these fascinating sites, the crop circles themselves began to become increasingly more elaborate and intricate.

Colin Andrews, one of the preeminent crop circle experts, reports that when he took people on crop circle tours, the crop circle that appeared the next day would often reflect the group consciousness. I remember one example he told of a group of Japanese visitors who asked if origami had ever appeared in a crop circle. Andrews told them no. The next day the first origami design appeared in a crop circle near where the Japanese group was staying.

Apparently there is an unconscious but two-way communication going on in crop circles. Perhaps that is why, as human consciousness becomes more interested in and studies crop circles, the circles themselves compensate with ever increasing degrees of complexity. And, like sacred sites, crop circles are meant to shift and elevate our awareness by using graceful and elegant images of beauty to stimulate us into higher resonance. They are meaningful, visual "toys" to capture our attention, make us wonder, and spend time contemplating them. And by doing so, our vibrational awareness grows in tandem. In other words, crop circles are created to increase our vibrational consciousness and evolution.

Mayan Calendar: The New Species Evolution Has Been Waiting For

—ɷ—

I'm here to tell you about good news! We all know about bad news. So much bad news, we can't take it in anymore. We turn our heads, distract our minds and hearts, because the bad news is so huge, so alarming, so pervasive, so seemingly impossible to fix, we tune out. "I'm just one person. What can I do?"

The good news I extrapolate from the Mayan Sacred Calendar—no, not the famous one that people say foretells doom and gloom. I mean the evolutionary Calendar of Consciousness.

It's a calendar not of time, but events. This Calendar tells us we're more than okay; we're evolving/evolved into a new species, one that is capable of conscious co-creation. The species that all of evolution has been planning, nurturing, and waiting for—us!

This Calendar is discussed brilliantly and clearly in books, videos (including on YouTube), and websites by both Carl Johan Calleman and Ian Xel Lungold. Calleman and Lungold have studied this Sacred Calendar for decades. They have found that important advances in human evolution

Universal (ninth)	Evolution of cosmic consciousness	Conscious co-creation	Feb. 11, 2011– Oct. 28, 2011
Galactic (eighth)	Evolution of galactic consciousness	Ethics	Jan. 5, 1999– Oct. 28, 2011
Planetary (seventh)	Evolution of global consciousness	Power	July 24, 1755– Oct. 28, 2011
National (sixth)	Evolution of civilized consciousness	Laws & Punishment	Aug. 11, 3115– Oct. 28, 2011
Regional (fifth)	Evolution of human consciousness	Complex tools, language, art	100,000 BC– Oct. 28, 2011
Tribal (fourth)	Evolution of hominid consciousness	First humans	2 million BC– Oct. 28, 2011
Familial (third)	Evolution of anthropoid consciousness	First primates	40 million BC– Oct. 28, 2011
Mammal (second)	Evolution mammalian consciousness	First animals	850 million BC– Oct. 28, 2011
Cellular (first)	Evolution of cellular consciousness	Big bang, galaxies, stars, higher cells	16.4 billion yrs.- Oct. 28, 2011

came during critical times of the Calendar that the Mayans "discovered" and brought to our attention.

To simplify—the Mayan Calendar of Consciousness goes through nine stages of evolution, starting with the big bang, through various evolutionary changes, until Oct. 28, 2011, when all nine stages culminated. At that point Mayan researchers believed that human beings, including our DNA and consciousness, evolved (or are evolving) into a brand-new species.

Who knows how the ancient Mayans figured this out? The bottom line for me is that their system follows the evolutionary process superbly through various stages (including timelines of millions and billions of years) from multi-celled organisms, to mammals, then primates, into humans, and continuing through human developments of reason, laws/punishment, power, ethics, and climaxing in conscious co-creation.

If one follows the Mayan system, there seems to be a "universal life vi-bration" that propels evolution forward, always advancing. The timing/energy/impetus is steadily and always in place to accelerate each phase of development to quicken and occur. This whole evolutionary process can be likened to a human being developing from newly-fertilized egg, to multi-cell organism, to embryo, to fetus, emerge as a fully-formed human being, then going through years of emotional, rational, verbal, and spiritual learning to mature into a functional member of the global society. It's as though Universal Energy is a Loving Parent, helping its "children" to form and mature into what we have been meant to become. This is an important concept to remember. We are meant to be here at this stage, at this phase, at this time, even with all our problems, to be a highly evolved species.

Perhaps problems are built in so that life can/must evolve. There were times in our planetary evolution that problems came along, and evolution shifted to (or was forced to follow) the path that was opened up by those very problems. Some examples:

—An excess of oxygen in the atmosphere, which forced anaerobic life forms to start breathing oxygen

—An event that killed off the dinosaurs, which made room for mammals and birds

—A climate change that decimated trees, which forced primates to move from living in jungles to savannahs, perhaps to walking upright

So maybe all along the way, life was assisted, even pushed or required to evolve. Evolve or die, as the saying goes. But I have a hunch there are invisible benign forces that have always been residing in the "nursery of evolution" to help us. If so, those forces are here still. Maybe because we cannot see or hear or sense them we feel alone, helpless, hopeless. But the Mayans tell us differently. "We will make it," say the Mayans. We are meant to make it. We (human beings, the earth, the universe, evolution itself) are designed to survive, develop, and—dare I say it—thrive! I know it doesn't look like it from our vantage point—yet. But my Council of Elders tells me every time I've asked—we're fine!

Here's one more possibility to cover, which I don't yet see on the Internet or Facebook, even with the spiritually aware folks. It's what Jung called the Collective UN-conscious. We are asked to love each other, forgive, be grateful, and practice mutual respect, and so on. That's all to the good. Yet all our work is on a CONSCIOUS level as we practice those worthy exercises.

As Rob Williams, the Founder of Psych-K, based on Dr. Bruce Lipton's work, says, our conscious mind is a very small percentage of our mind. The UN-conscious mind is where the majority of our mind resides. And often we can't do anything about that unconscious mind.

"...The interaction between mind, body and spirit has a profound influence on how we feel....but unconscious beliefs which we are not even aware of impact us every day. Psych-K, short for Psychological Kinesiology, is [a]... treatment option that allows us bring the unconscious beliefs that are negatively impacting our health out into the option to affect a lasting change...Most of our brain is devoted to unconscious thought, and it is these unconscious thoughts and beliefs we have about ourselves that can have such a negative effect on our health. In a groundbreaking book, *The Biology of Belief*, cellular biologist Dr. Bruce Lipton describes our beliefs as a form of energy that affects the cell membrane, creating health or disease within our cells."—*https://www.psych-k.com/*

I'm taking this one step further than Lipton or Williams. As I've said, humans are part of what Jung calls the Collective UN-conscious. According to quantum physicists nowadays, we (humans *and* nature) are all connected as one. The physicists call it non-locality or quantum entanglement. Einstein called it "spooky action at a distance." Our collective unconscious is connected, entangled together. Although it is probably helpful to practice conscious affirmations and behaviors of love, harmony, and so on, it is our COLLECTIVE mind that is running our global show.

We are all connected: peacemakers and terrorists, liberals and conservatives, all religions, all people, sick or healthy, everywhere —AND—at the same time we are connected immutably to all of nature—the soil, plants, animals, sky, air, water. So does that mean our collective unconscious includes nature? It must, if physicists are correct. And it's not just physicists, but indigenous wisdom, and metaphysical tradition, that says "everything is connected to everything." There is no "Them" out there who are creating problems, it is "Us," our collective unconscious. By the way, there is no blame involved. We are simply learning and growing.

This could be good news or bad news. I prefer to believe the Mayans and their Sacred Calendar and call it good news. Somehow at this moment in time we are evolving, changing, and growing, into a new highly-conscious species, one that will be aware and respectful of our connection to one another, all of nature, and all of the universe. One that will consider the preciousness of every drop of water, every person, every flower and insect, as if each of them is oneself. I believe this is happening automatically. Right now, as a matter of fact. Maybe it doesn't look like it. But perhaps these are the very problems leading to the solutions and our evolution.

Whatever looks like a problem can/will be easily resolved from our new consciousness. And that consciousness includes nature. Nature can solve some of our most intractable problems—like fungi that loves to eat plastic, mushrooms that clean polluted, even irradiated water and soil, and man-made floating plant islands that transform polluted water into pristine lakes, rivers, and streams. We can and must make nature our full partner—as our teacher, not our subject.

I recently came across a phrase, and can't remember from whom, that sums up my whole discussion nicely: "the universe is self-organizing and self-evolving." What the Mayans have taught us is that we're fine. We're on the proper course of our evolution right now. The universe could not have painstakingly created all of these steps of evolution as iterated in the Sacred Mayan Calendar, only to slam shut the evolutionary door in our face at the last moment.

Therefore, I and the Mayan Calendar researchers believe we're at the culmination point of the Mayan Sacred Calendar where humans are becoming a new species, one that consciously co-creates with the universe. What looks like bad news is just GOOD NEWS ready to happen. News at 11:00.

No One Is To Blame For Our Problems

I see a lot of problems here on our planet. But there's no one to blame for those problems. Not you. Not me. Not the Illuminati or the Bankers or Politicians or some Other Religion or even God.

"Everything is perfect, no matter what it looks like. For the purpose of growth, learning and evolution," say my Council of Elders.

We are all here together in one big Group Consciousness. We learn and grow together.

As time has gone by, we human beings learned. We learned religion. We learned building. We learned growing food. We learned technology. Most of us believed that the planet belonged to us. That we were the sovereign masters over all we saw. We wanted to control nature and each other. We wanted to invent things. We wanted energy to further improve our lifestyles. We wanted money to do things and buy things and see things. All of us wanted more than we had, for ourselves, our families, or others. There is no fault in any of those wants. We were like eager children, ready to head over the horizon to the next frontier, the next tomorrow, often without realizing the costs.

Now we see that all our wanting and learning has brought us to where we are now. Not all of it is bad. We didn't mean to hurt each other or the planet or animals or nature. We got ahead of ourselves. Our consciousness didn't keep up with advanced technology, especially weaponry. But there's no one to blame for it.

Many people are now awakening. They look around and are aghast. "It must have been someone OUT THERE who did this."

We simply weren't paying attention. But we are now. Now we are learning and growing. The very problems that upset us are the impetus to compel us to new learning.

I spend many nights lying in bed, practicing forgiveness, being grateful to everyone, especially those whom I might otherwise want to blame. But blame doesn't make me feel better. And blame doesn't solve problems either. Now we can learn cooperation. The ten trillion cells in our body know how to cooperate and work together. We can too.

I find that gratitude especially brings me to peace and happiness. I'm not saying it's easy. I'm not even saying that I believed my own words when I first started saying them out loud. But more and more, with repetition, the forgiveness, love, and gratitude towards others is shifting my attitudes, my life, and even my physical body.

Perhaps this seems counter-intuitive to you. All I know is when I remove blame and finger-pointing from the equation, the equation begins to shift. Subtly at first, then stronger and stronger. Blame is the old paradigm and it's time for the new.

The Conduits' To-Do List

E verthing is perfect, no matter what it looks like—for the purpose of learning, growing, healing, and evolving. Everthing is perfect, no matter what it looks like—— no matter if it changes or not.

Everthing is perfect...for the good of all concerned.
I am grateful for the pain.
This pain is not mine.
I am grateful for the thoughts.
The thoughts are not mine.
I am grateful for the headache.
This headache is not mine.
I am grateful for the emotions.
The emotions are not mine.
I am grateful for the body.
This body is not mine.
I am grateful for the confusion.
The confusion is not mine.

I am grateful for the fatigue.

The fatigue is not mine.

I am grateful for having a body.

The body is not my body.

The body is the means through which I am helping the planet, 144,000 at a time.

I am grateful for being a Conduit.

A Conduit is the grace for which I neutralize and heal anything that is not love.

The body and the emotions heal because I am a Conduit.

My karma dissolves because I am a Conduit.

I am grateful for the planet.

The planet works its miracles with my help. The planet heals because I am a Conduit.

I love to do my job. I am grateful to help.

The universe is grateful for my help.

Love, Gratitude, Forgiveness, and Peace come through my body for me and all those to whom I'm attached.

Whatever spiritual lessons I learn, those lessons are sent through this Conduit to those 144,000 people who adopt it as theirs. Whatever spiritual happiness those people have, they return that happiness to me.

I am ascending into the fifth dimension because I do the work of a Conduit. I am delighted to be participating in my job of Conduit. I learn and grow with every piece of energy that flows through me that is healed and neutralized. I am thrilled to be part of the growth of the planet. I am thrilled to be a Conduit.

Every day, in every way, I am floating above problems, seeing only peace, forgiveness, gratitude, love, and happiness in those problems. The problems shift in my mind's eye into spiritual energy.

Tea With Bin Laden (a true story)

—∽∽—

’m sure you remember where you were and what you were doing on that fateful morning in September 2001. I was sound asleep when Paul called on the phone and woke me up.

"Lauren, turn on the TV," he said, his voice solemn. Paul never called me Lauren unless he wanted to talk about something serious. "Lauren, I think the next war has started. Planes are bombing the Trade Center."

"What?!" I was suddenly awake. Memories of hundreds of nightmares I've had since I was a kid returned in full force. "I'll call you back." I hung up the phone, ran into the living room, and turned on the TV. My son and his wife were sleeping on a bed there. They were staying with me until Nathan could find a new job, having lost a position and without means at the time.

"Ma!" Nathan complained, turning over in bed. "What's up? It's really early."

"I know, honey," I answered him. "But something is wrong. Planes are bombing the trade center." I turned the volume up.

Then began the minute by minute, hour by hour reporting, and then replaying—a jet crashing into the south tower of the World Trade Center.

The north tower was already on fire, flames and smoke pouring out. Soon the Pentagon would be hit. Then United Airlines Flight 93 would crash near Shanksville, Pennsylvia. Finally, the nearly-instantaneous collapse of three buildings, while Nathan, Luz, and I watched horrified, unable to move, eat breakfast, or even think coherently. Those scenes are indelibly burned into communal memories all over our planet while that day marked the end of an era and the beginning of a new one. The news announcers told us that Al-Qaeda was to blame for the attacks, the mastermind of that organization being Osama Bin Laden.

I had been a spiritual pilgrim to sacred sites for a few years, then returning home and writing articles about my metaphysical and spiritual experiences while there. I had, with the help of Paul's grandson Corey, created a website. It consisted of my many articles, both on sacred sites and general spiritual subjects, as well as a free site to find metaphysical tours to sacred sites worldwide. I charged nothing, neither to visitors nor the 104 tour companies I listed. It was my gift to the Universe.

I had been immersed in my own spiritual world, quite unaware of political, national, or global news for decades. My avoidance had started when I was in my twenties, when I had been watching coverage of the Vietnam war on the television every night. I felt emotionally torn apart watching that terrible carnage, and finally turned off the news, not turning it on again until 9/11.

While Nathan and Luz continued to watch, hour after hour, I felt that I had to do something, anything, to bring a spiritual balance to the awfulness that had invaded our living room and our lives. I went into my bedroom, closed my eyes, and began to chant over and over for what seemed like an eternity:

"I bless all the people who have died.
I bless the firefighters.
I bless the police officers.
I bless the onlookers.

I bless Mayor Giuliani.

I bless all the helpers.

I bless our government.

I bless President Bush.

I bless the American people.

I bless our troops.

I bless the world.

I bless Al-Qaeda.

I bless Bin Laden."

Performing the blessings made me feel a little saner, as though the world hadn't suddenly fallen out of its orbit around the sun.

Then I would begin again:

"I bless all the people who have died.

I bless the firefighters…"etc., etc.

What I was doing may sound repugnant to you. After all, we were taught to hate Bin Laden and the terrorists. But my Council of Elders, a group of Ascended Masters who have worked with me since I was five years old, had years before taught me an important mantra: "Everything is perfect, no matter what it looks like, for the purpose of learning, growth, and evolving."

The Elders come from a highly advanced consciousness of enlightenment, one that is difficult for us human beings to comprehend with our limited awareness and logical, egoist minds. In fact, the mantra could seem like a contradiction, a conundrum, like a Buddhist Koan. Yet their mantra often brought me great peace. With that in mind, 9/11 was perfect, for humanity to learn, grow, and evolve from the tragedy.

So there I was on the morning of 9/11. I evoked the Elders, reminded once again that everything was perfect. If that is the case, then the terrorists and Bin Laden are perfect, too. And so I chanted all day. It was the only thing that kept me from sobbing in despair and grief.

I found that, as I chanted "I bless…" the individuals that I blessed seemed to soak up the blessing like a healing balm. (The only one who rejected my blessing was President Bush.)

Even Bin Laden was happy to receive my blessing.

The first night, the evening of 9/11, Bin Laden's energy appeared to me while I was chanting, and interrupted me.

"You're an American," he said, more as a question.

"Yes, I am," I replied quietly, a little surprised at his appearance.

"Are you a Muslim?" he asked me.

"No, I'm not,".

"Then why are you blessing me?" Bin Laden asked, rather heatedly it seemed to me.

I thought for a moment, and then answered, "Because you are my brother. You live on planet earth, and we are connected as a planetary family." It seemed logical to me.

I could feel him rolling that idea around in his mind, yet his "brow" furrowed. "But. . . doesn't your country hate me?"

"I suppose so," I replied. "But I don't."

"Why don't you?" he asked again.

I took a deep breath and let it out. "Because…you are my spiritual brother and we must all learn to get along."

I could feel his impatience and non-understanding as Bin Laden's energy left my space.

I was pretty worn out, emotionally, physically, and psychologically, as most of us were that day. I was also saturated with the repeating images of the planes and buildings and suggested we go out to eat. During dinner Nathan proposed a plan of us buying special tires for my truck, going shopping for food and guns, then heading out to the country. I told him I didn't want to do that. But he persisted in his planning through the meal. We all went to bed early that night.

I no longer chanted after that first day, but kept the idea of blessing everyone uppermost in my mind.

The next night Bin Laden's energy (or soul/spirit) showed up again, asking the same questions.

"Are you an American?"

"Yes."

"Are you a Muslim?"

"No."

"Why are you blessing me?"

"Because you are my brother and I would rather love than hate you."

He disappeared once again.

The third evening, just as I had gone to bed, Bin Laden returned. This time was a little different. He "invited" me to join him at tea. I followed him to a dimly lit, damp, dark little "home." I sat down at an old wooden table. It was just the two of us as he poured me some mint tea and I "sipped" the tea, waiting for his inevitable questions.

"Are you an American?"

"Yes."

"Are you a Muslim?"

"No."

Now he seemed very disturbed and leaned towards me. "Then I just don't understand why you would bless me." I could feel his confusion and a desire to comprehend my point of view.

I tried very hard to make my point. "I believe we are all related on this planet as human beings. The Elders tell me that everything and everyone is connected, like the physicists say. So that means that you are my brother." I paused.

"But why do you not reject me, as the others in your country have?"

"I can't speak for them. I can only speak for myself. I want there to be peace, between you and me, among all of us. We need to learn to love each other, to stop war and hatred."

"But you are not a Muslim," he persisted.

"No, I'm not."

With that, he imperiously waved his hand, and I was dismissed from the table and his life forever.

I have told this story a lot through the years. It always makes me wonder how I even thought to chant what I did. To include Bin Laden and al-Qaeda in my blessings. I am further amazed that Bin Laden came to visit me, to question my activity. But then I have had many unusual experiences in my life. The unusual feels normal to me!

I believe the same way today as then. We are all related by our spiritual heritage. We all reside on this planet. We all struggle to learn, take care of our families, to live our lives as best we can.

If we don't love one another, bless each other, we are doomed to war, hatred, revenge, and perhaps annihilation.

As Tiny Tim says in Dickens' *Christmas Carol,* "Bless us all....Every One."

Pay Attention: Your Well-Being Depends On Being A Good Psychic

—⚬—

I believe that all humans are intuitive, psychic, have extra-sensory perceptions. I believe that our inborn, intuitive abilities are vital to our well-being, health, careers, maybe our lives. I hope this article will encourage you to hone your abilities, regardless if you are just beginning or have been practicing for many years.

I've talked to some successful people. One thing those people had in common is what they call "gut feelings" or "instincts" when it comes to knowing who to trust or when to sign that important deal.

When learning to become a good psychic, the first and most important requirement is to PAY ATTENTION. I mean pay attention to everything. What you see. What you hear. What you feel, smell, taste. What you imagine that you feel, smell, or taste. When your hair stands on end or you get goose bumps (I call them truth-bumps) or you just KNOW.

You need to pay attention at all times during the day and night. When you're by yourself. When you're with others. When you're tired; when you're alert. When you're driving, or as a passenger. When you're watching TV or a movie, listening to music, the radio or to someone else speak. When you're at work. When you're at home or out in public. You must pay attention to everything. Every nuance. Especially the things that don't seem to have any overt meaning at all.

You can visualize the stereotype of a Native American we've seen in movies. You know, those depictions of an American Indian getting off his horse to closely examine something on the ground. To sniff it. Examine it. Track it. To know the difference between the scent of a deer or that of a bear. You can aspire to be that noble native. This is in spite of the fact you haven't been trained as natives once were. You must train yourself to intuit messages in every leaf, stone, word, smell, news report, and personal interaction. Everything is important, as you will learn.

You must be willing to appear ridiculous. Others may not be picking up what you do. Others may even make fun of you, if you tell them what you're picking up. But ultimately you will possess a special talent to rely on. To intuit messages only you can hear. This talent can protect you and others in simple and also amazing ways.

IGNORE the logical mind. You can trust your senses in becoming intuitive—NOT your logic. The logical mind will try to talk you out of your message. For example the mind will say: "That's ridiculous." "That doesn't make any sense." "I must be tired, or anxious, or have an over-active imagination." "I'm just being judgmental." The logical mind is good for balancing your checkbook or doing your job—but not for psychic information.

Your logical mind may try to convince you otherwise—but pay no attention. In fact, when I am guiding clients on "past life journeys" I tell them to leave the logical mind behind. If they get stuck and can't remember details, I tell them to "make it up." It disengages the logical mind and takes them directly to their intuition.

You will discover the method(s) in which you best pick up messages: whether it is seeing (clairvoyance); hearing (clairaudience); sensing (clairsentience); knowing (claircognizance); tasting (clairgustance); smelling (clairtangency); or a combination.

Psychics know it's of utmost importance to pay attention to that silly little thought that pops into your head out of nowhere. The thought says "You …" as though someone separate from you is talking to you. You may only get one chance to pay attention to that thought. If it's extremely urgent, you may get the message again—but often it won't repeat. Sometimes when I intuit something significant, it sounds like "bells and whistles" go off in my head, which is hard to ignore. I don't ignore them anymore. The same is true for instant gut feelings and visions. You may even be able to "sniff out" danger. Pay attention to them all.

Your messages may come in the form of dreams. So if you dream something important, pay attention.

Next you must TRUST whatever you get—implicitly. You must trust yourself even WHEN or IF others are telling you that you are wrong or dumb or crazy. If you intuit, you must stick to your integrity, no matter what. A smooth life, relationships, and career depend on your messages. It could even be a case of life or death.

Finally, depending on what you discern, you may need to take AC-TION. This is sometimes the hardest part. Taking action can sometimes feel like standing at the edge of a sheer cliff, with nothing below but empty space, while your message insists that you jump. I will elaborate this below in stories #3 and #4.

STORY 1: I sometimes ignore instructions, like "take your sweater with you" when it is hot out, only to have the weather cool suddenly.

But the time that I remember with horrifying clarity was when I was on a casual date decades ago. I was twenty years old. I didn't know the man I was with well. I was driving my car that night. He told me there was a party and directed me to the house, which seemed dark and un-inviting as we pulled up. I didn't want to go in but he concocted a story that others would arrive soon. Although I had "bells and whistles" going off in my head, and a terrible premonition in my gut, I went in the house anyway.

The result of ignoring that message was I got raped.

I don't ignore "bells and whistles" anymore!

STORY 2: Sometimes I get a message and I don't know exactly what it means until later. A dear friend I worked with wanted to date a new employee (I'll call him Jack) in our county social services office. Instantly I had a bad feeling, although I hadn't paid any attention to the man before. "Don't date him," I advised her. "You'll be sorry."

Next an office mate mentioned Jack in an admiring tone. "Isn't he handsome?"

Just as suddenly as before, I blurted out emphatically, "I wouldn't trust Jack as far as I could throw him!"

Some days later the Office Manager brought me in to talk about Jack. I told her my reactions, and she replied she was having bad feelings about Jack, too. She trusted my intuition (and her own) and had Jack followed by investigators. What turned up is that Jack had undertaken many criminal actions in his job among which he embezzled money from the county, acted as pimp for some of his female clients, and had perpetuated the same kind of criminal activity in other counties, too. He wasn't a citizen and was deported to a country in Africa, where his father was imprisoned as a political prisoner. Jack would suffer the same fate. It's amazing what our intuitions can pick up, seemingly out of nowhere.

STORY 3: I had been married for seven years. He was step-father to my two children, and was a kind man. I loved him deeply, although we had many marital problems. One day I was getting a massage from a friend of mine, Kathy. I gave Kathy psychic counseling in exchange for therapeutic massage once a week. This particular day, in the middle of her soothing massage, I heard the following message inside my head: "Leave Tom now." I opened my eyes and told Kathy what I heard. I puzzled over it but didn't think anything more about it.

The following week I was again getting a massage from Kathy. I got the same message only this time it was louder and more imperative: "Leave your husband. Now!!"

I wasn't going to ignore the second message. I went home and told him I was divorcing him. He asked me why I was leaving, but I wasn't able to give him a good explanation.

I moved myself and my two children to a new home within the week. After we had moved in, and we were unpacking, my twelve-year-old daughter came to me, thanking me for moving away from Tom. She explained that around the time of the first message (which she didn't know about), Tom had started molesting her! Consciously I didn't "know" anything, but I was grateful to have paid attention to—and took action—on the psychic messages.

STORY 4: I have received numerous intuitions over the span of my lifetime, but I'm only going to tell you one final story, about timing. TIMING is all-important in many messages. Timing is all-important in the universe.

Paul and I had bought a farm and worked it for eight years. It was exhausting work, but we persevered. At one point we thought about selling it and went to a realtor. The realtor told us we could get far less profit for it than we hoped. This was during the economic downturn and housing crisis; everyone was having problems selling property. She also showed us pictures of what we could get for our money. The houses and neighborhoods weren't what we wanted to live in, in fact, they were downright ugly. So we struggled on for another year.

One day in June 2011, "out of the blue" I got the message, "Sell the farm now!" I didn't hesitate. I sent out many emails advertising our farm, without the means of a realtor. The next day a couple showed up and gave us a full-price offer. The sale and escrow went through smoothly and we took our profits, and moved to a lovely house in a great neighborhood. Everyone who knew us believed our sale was a miracle. I knew it was simply a message. My message was and always is—pay attention!

What On Earth Is the Sun Doing To Us?

—ɯɯ—

For most of my life I thought of the sun as just a big ball of fire in the sky, warming our bodies, growing plants, and sometimes giving me sunburn.

Then one day in January 2012, when I was discussing the mysterious and abrupt comings-and-goings of my physical, mental, and psychological shifts with a new friend, she conveyed information about solar flares with me. She told me about her naturopath, who tracks solar flares for her patients and their illnesses.

I was fascinated and curious. I located an internet site called *SpaceWeather.com*, which tracks these mysterious bursts of energy from our local star. That website keeps a daily log on sunspots, solar flares, and something called Coronal Mass Ejections (CME's). I have been going to *SpaceWeather.com* every day, correlating how I was feeling versus what the sun was doing.

I have been following solar activity daily since the beginning of February 2012. Although I haven't kept a written record, when solar activity was high, I had many unexplained symptoms (see list below) within 18 to 24 hours of the blast leaving the sun, and the effects lasted one to four days, depending on the magnitude of the CME. Some of the symptoms were so severe I went to my doctor, who performed tests, but revealed nothing wrong with me. The Carlini Institute for Therapy, Research, and Transpersonal Education reports inconclusive doctor visits as well.

I also noticed that when the sun is quiet, meaning less sunspot activity, fewer flares or CME's, I feel well, happy, and energetic, without many physical, mental, or psychological symptoms.

When I checked with my friends, they reported symptoms in quite a similar way and with comparable timing. Because of that, I started posting solar alerts on my Facebook page. A number of Facebook friends have thanked me for doing so and for educating them about solar weather effects.

Once in a while (maybe ten percent of the time) when the Earth was subjected to flares or CME's, I didn't have any noticeable effects. This confused me. Then as I was watching a documentary, *Secrets of the Sun,* produced by PBS/NOVA, a scientist gave a suitable explanation for the difference. The Earth is magnetically charged (positive to negative) and so is a CME. If the CME hits the Earth with a particular charge, let's say positive, and hits the positive field of the sun, the effect is nil, just as two magnets would repel each other if similarly placed together. And the opposite is true—when the CME's magnetic charge is opposite to that of the Earth, we then feel strong effects.

To briefly explain the working of the sun—our star consists of hot plasma interwoven with magnetic fields.

> *"The sun has 11-year cycles of sunspots and intense magnetic storms followed by predictable periods of quiet. We are now into a new cycle that is expected to be 30 to 50 percent stronger than the previous one according to Mausumi Dikpati of the National Center for Atmospheric Research (NCAR) in Boulder, Colorado."* —CarliniInstitute.com
>
> *"The key to the mystery [of the cycles], Dikpati realized years ago, is a conveyor belt on the sun. "The sun's conveyor belt is a current of elec-*

trically-conducting gas. It flows in a loop from the sun's equator to the poles and back again. Just as the Great Ocean Conveyor Belt controls weather on Earth, this solar conveyor belt controls weather on the sun. Specifically, it controls the sunspot cycle." —Universe Today

The sun is a complex celestial body consisting of layers of gas. Energy arises from the deepest layer, until it materializes on the surface, with energy the equivalent of one trillion megaton bombs every second! Sun spots are an active, bubbling stew of newly-arrived radiation on the sun's surface, consisting of protons, x-rays, gamma waves, radio waves, and geo-magnetic fields. This radiation is then taken up by the Conveyer Belt. Energy is constantly flowing out of the sun into space as the solar wind, buffeting Earth and the planets in our solar system. Often it erupts in the form of solar flares. Less often it bursts free in the form of a CME. A CME is categorized as C-class, M-class and X-class.

"A solar flare is an explosion on the Sun that happens when energy stored in twisted magnetic fields (usually above sunspots) is suddenly released. Flares produce a burst of radiation across the electromagnetic spectrum, from radio waves to x-rays and gamma-rays. Scientists classify solar flares according to their x-ray brightness in the wavelength range 1 to 8 Angstroms. There are 3 categories: X-class flares are big; they are major events that can trigger planet-wide radio blackouts and long-lasting radiation storms. M-class flares are medium-sized; they can cause brief radio blackouts that affect Earth's polar regions. Minor radiation storms sometimes follow an M-class flare. Compared to X- and M-class events, C-class flares are small with few noticeable consequences here on Earth." —Spaceweather.com

Depending on the direction the sun is facing, away from Earth or towards Earth, a CME may harmlessly explode into space, not affecting Earth. Or it can send its torrent of plasma towards Earth at enormous speed, arriving hours later. What the atmospheric scientists tell us is that the bigger and/or more active the sunspot, the more likely we are to have major solar flares or higher class CME's.

> *"One of the biggest sunspots in years, AR1520, is turning toward Earth. Christian Viladrich of Nattages, France, photographed the behemoth on July 7th. It looks like an expanse of land on the sun, says Viladrich. Despite the resemblance to land, however, the vast dark cores of sunspot AR1520 are not solid. They are made of magnetism. Each one is a magnetic island nearly as wide as Earth floating in a sea of solar plasma. Sunspot AR1520 is 200,000 miles of an island chain. The magnetic field of this enormous sunspot harbors energy for strong solar flares. NOAA forecasters estimate an 80% chance of M-flares and a 25% chance of X-flares."* Spaceweather.com July 10, 2012

The Earth has a protective magnetic shield surrounding it, without which we would be cooked to a cinder, our atmosphere burnt up, as in the case of Mars. Global Coherence Initiative—also known as Heart Math (*https://www.heartmath.org/gci/*)—is collecting data and joining forces on how we humans can collectively strengthen our weakening Interplanetary Magnetic Field.

When solar wind, solar flares, or CME's arrive at Earth, they hit the protective layer, and then effervesce through the Earth's magnetosphere. The solar energy often shows up visually as beautifully dancing aurora borealis (northern lights), usually in the far northern latitudes. In June, 2012, however, during an intense CME, the northern lights showed up as far south as Nebraska. Recently the aurora appeared simultaneously in both the north AND south poles, which is unusual.

> *Sometimes auroras are not due to an explosion from the sun, but rather "a fluctuation in the Interplanetary Magnetic Field (IMF). On July 9, 2012, the IMF near Earth tipped south, opening our planet's magnetosphere."* —Spaceweather.com, July 11, 2012

The effects are the same, however. Solar wind poured in through the opening in the magnetospher, and ignited the northern lights in Canada and the South Pole.

The Sun spews billions of tons of plasma into space periodically, containing x-rays, gamma rays, and other geo-magnetic waves of energy. And those energies affect us on Earth in ways that are shocking.

Traditional scientists report that solar flares and CME's only affect satellites, the electric grid, cell phones, microwaves, and other electronic instruments. They collectively believe that solar flares DO NOT affect human beings, animals, or influence natural phenomenon like earthquakes and volcanic activity.

I disagree, at least about humans. The Carlini Institute for Therapy, Research, and Transpersonal Education, which has been studying these effects on humans for years, has an extensive list of reported effects:

> *"Solar flares affect the Central Nervous System (stomach lining), all brain activity (including equilibrium), along with human behavior and all psycho-physiological (mental-emotional- physical) response. Solar flares can cause us to be nervous, anxiousness, worrisome, jittery, dizzy, shaky, irritable, lethargic, exhausted, have short term memory problems, feel nauseous, queasy, and to have prolonged head pressure and headaches…migraines; the inability to think straight; losing words in the middle of a thought; ringing in the ears; exhaustion…stomach aches; indigestion; loss of appetite or wanting to eat incessantly; heart palpitations; irregular heartbeats; vertigo; face going red…heat sensations felt in the body…feeling cold for no reason…dreams that are different from…[normal]…dreams."* —© Heather Carlini, 2010, 2011, 2012, CarliniInstitute.com

In fact, it is because of my personal exploration that I am writing this article at all. I muddle along as a non-scientific person, yet with a mission to inform you of what I have discovered. According to most of the scientists

I have read or heard, we are expected to have 30% to 50% more solar activity, at least for this current solar cycle. I noticed that since September 2011, I am having symptoms more often and more intensely. I also noticed that even when a CME "misses" Earth and storms out into space, I still get symptoms. I have no explanation for that, except perhaps I am overly sensitive. Or perhaps scientists don't yet fully understand the sun's activities. No wonder ancient people credited the sun as a god.

What does higher solar activity mean for us here on Earth in the future? We'll see.

Meanwhile, we can keep track and determine if there is a correlation, and whether or not our many incongruous symptoms are based on the activity of our nearest sun.

** Global Coherence Initiative is collecting data on how we humans can collectively strengthen our now-weakening Interplanetary Magnetic Field.

8th Level Evolution of
Human Consciousness: Ethics

—⟐—

Part 1: What is the Ethical Level of Consciousness?
How Did We Get Here?

I've spent a lot of time writing about the Ninth and ultimate evolution of human consciousness according to the Mayan Calendar, which is CONSCIOUS CO-CREATION.[1] Yet I've noticed that many people are "stuck" for lack of a better word, at the Eighth level, which is ETHICS. Both of these levels are recent developments.

Human consciousness (according to Carl Calleman) began to wrap its group mind around what Ethics is, and what it means for global existence, a mere twelve years ago. The Eighth level began on January 5, 1999 and culminated on October 28, 2011 (a total of 12.8 years). The Ninth level began on February 11, 2011 and culminated on October 28, 2011, for a total of just 260 days. That means incredibly recent advances in the span of human consciousness are thrusting us swiftly into new realms. We are hurrying to catch up with ourselves.

Prior to these aspects of consciousness we had two others levels—Sixth and Seventh. The Sixth had to do with learning about LAWS & PUNISH-MENT (August 11, 3115 BC–2011 AD—laws of governance and abiding by laws), while the Seventh taught us about POWER (July 24, 1755–2011—which includes revolutions and emergence of national countries)

Universal (ninth)	Evolution of cosmic consciousness	Conscious co-creation	Feb. 11, 2011–Oct. 28, 2011
Galactic (eighth)	Evolution of galactic consciousness	Ethics	Jan. 5, 1999–Oct. 28, 2011
Planetary (seventh)	Evolution of global consciousness	Power	July 24, 1755–Oct. 28, 2011
National (sixth)	Evolution of civilized consciousness	Laws & Punishment	Aug. 11, 3115–Oct. 28, 2011
Regional (fifth)	Evolution of human consciousness	Complex tools, language, art	100,000 BC–Oct. 28, 2011
Tribal (fourth)	Evolution of hominid consciousness	First humans	2 million BC–Oct. 28, 2011
Familial (third)	Evolution of anthropoid consciousness	First primates	40 million BC–Oct. 28, 2011
Mammal (second)	Evolution mammalian consciousness	First animals	850 million BC–Oct. 28, 2011
Cellular (first)	Evolution of cellular consciousness	Big bang, galaxies, stars, higher cells	16.4 billion yrs.-Oct. 28, 2011

Why are these dates important? If you study the chart above, you will see that each rung on the ladder of consciousness is shorter than the rung before it. The first rung took 16.4 billion years. When we get to the Eighth rung, we see that consciousness (of ethics) has sped up, beginning and terminating in approximately 11 years, a phenomenal, exponential rate of growth. Consider the internet and computers, which have helped in that short evolution.

As we ascended the nine rungs of the Pyramid of Consciousness, Calleman postulates that we learned about, and then incorporated, that which came before, like the steps of human development from a baby to an adult. As you can tell, we humans pretty much understand the consciousness of Laws/Punishment and Power and have incorporated these into our civilizations.

Now, however, we are struggling to integrate Ethics into our awareness. It's only recently that, with the help of a new invention, the Internet, we have begun to uncover unethical behavior all around us—in government, politics, business, banking, NASA, CIA, the media, Big Pharma, to name just a few, at global, national, and personal levels. Stories are constantly emerging of yet more unethical behavior. I believe those discoveries and disclosures of unethical behavior are important, as we wrestle with comprehending and integrating the meaning and texture of Ethics into human existence. In other words, Power isn't bad per se. There's no one to blame for unethical abuses of Power, because it is part of our group learning and growth. We simply need to move forward and change our behavior.

Are these unethical behaviors a recent development? Or has unethical behavior been going on all along and we haven't been aware of it? Or is unethical behavior forcing us to become more ethical?

As I see it, today's Ethics are set against the background of consciousness' earlier development—Power and earlier still, Laws. Power and Laws without Ethics have no integrity and collapse under their own weight, as we can see everywhere in the world today. Why didn't it break down earlier?

What is Ethical anyway? My thesaurus states ethics also means: moral, principles, right, decent, proper, fitting, virtuous, just, honorable, upright, and fair. I prefer to live in a world where these virtues are common practice. Don't you? I prefer to live in a world where these virtues are common practice. Don't you?

How can we run businesses and countries using ethical behavior? How do we assimilate Ethics into Laws and Power? Do we need to rewrite laws, redo human development, teach our children early? These are weighty questions, ones appropriate to our time, and relevant to each individual's development, as well as our collective.

Earlier, when I said we are "stuck" at the Eighth level, I mean some individuals and groups spend a great deal of time and energy pointing out and fighting against unethical behavior. They get angry, rant, demonstrate, and produce documentaries. Not that anger, ranting, and demonstrating are bad, but are perhaps outmoded and, in some sense, overdone. I can't listen to the stories anymore. I am saturated to the breaking point.

"What?" you may exclaim. "Lauren, group dissent is practically institutionalized behavior. In the past, we created rights, amendments, and more just laws, by doing those things!"

"I realize that," I reply. But that was the past. We are now in the present. Consciousness has changed. We live in a different universe now. In fact, since October 28, 2011, we have even zoomed beyond Ethics to include Conscious Co-Creation.

We are being pressured by universal intelligence into formulating and dispensing Ethics. We don't need to focus on what ISN'T ethical. Rather we can focus on what IS ethical, given our new understandings. Then we can blend Ethics into Laws and Power into our lives. And ultimately we can stir our Consciousness Stew into Conscious Co-Creation and create what we want.

Part 2: How to Take Ethical Action For Yourself

I have been practicing this for awhile now. What I have discovered is this:

All consciousness begins with the individual. You are in charge of yourself and your own personal universe. What you do makes a difference, both personally and in the big picture. Think of the Hundreth Monkey.

If you find yourself being victimized by unethical, illegal, criminal, or other unhelpful behavior from a company, corporation (no matter how big and intimidating, including doctors and dentists), retail stores (brick-and-mortar or internet), or even an individual, identify the problem in detail.

In your own personal life, you *can* do something. Forgo being a victim and eliminate victim consciousness. You must become your own advocate.

You can let go of your anger and hostility, and remain calm. You now have the Universe on your side, so you don't have to "fight" anymore. You can "float."

You can write down your grievances and complaints.

You can brainstorm and then write down how you want your grievance resolved. Sometimes you simply want to lodge a complaint. Other times, you may want money back, a refund, an apology, or some other solution. Be creative. Ask for what you WANT.

If you start with a phone call to the unethical business, keep notes. Remain polite and courteous—and FIRM. Record the date, who you talked to (full name if possible), what was discussed, and details of a resolution. Get the company's phone number, address, the name of administrators or owner, email address, and toll-free number. Tell the person what you expect to happen. See if a resolution occurs as a result of your phone call.

If an initial phone call isn't helpful to resolve your grievance, you can send a letter with copies of attachments and enclosures to the business or corporation with a CC (copy) to other helpful agencies. Remain polite and courteous. Be sure to let the original business know that you are sending copies to other agencies (if you are). Sending a physical letter(s) is more powerful than emails or phone calls, which can easily be ignored, deleted, or lost.

Locate and use other agencies to help you if necessary. The Internet is a great resource for this.

The most important agency to contact for all grievances is the Attorney General in your state, who will open a case and act as a mediator for your grievance, including sending a letter to the offending company. The Attorney General tracks grievances and may even initiate a Class Action Suit against a company that regularly practices unethical business behavior. It's helpful to have the Big Dogs on your side.

If you believe that the company was using criminal tactics, like "bait and switch" or confidence schemes ("if you send us money for… , we'll give you a job/cash/make you rich, put money into your bank account"), ridiculous promises that they fail to fulfill, false advertising, or coerce you into paying more money that you didn't sign up for (cell phone companies use this strategy), then you can send a CC to your local police department, Chamber of Commerce, and Better Business Bureau. The BBB also acts as a mediator in grievances. That makes two Big Dogs in your corner.

If your complaint regards a doctor, dentist, therapist, or other medical organization, you can send a CC to your State's Medical Association, Association of Psychotherapy, AMA, or others you may think would be helpful or who might want to know. There may be a watchdog association tracking unethical medical practices you can locate.

If you believe you need a lawyer to help you, you can contact one. Ask for a free consultation.

You may not get any or all of what you ask for in this process. But you won't get anything if you don't ask. I get satisfaction from knowing I stood up for myself. Anything else is a bonus. The more we lodge complaints and take action, I more I believe the unethical methods will begin to crumble, to be replaced by ethical standards.

Part 3: The Challenge to Live in the Ethical Dimension

The challenge as I envision it is for personal, interpersonal, and global integrity. I have an image of nesting circles including each one of us, our communities, the nations, and the world. Ever-expanding circles of relationships in which we are all as conscious as possible, and eternally vigilant.

Am I acting in an ethical manner? Is there an ethical action I/we can take? What does it mean to live in an ethical dimension, make ethical choices?

Ultimately this means individual responsibility for one's own actions, thoughts, feelings, and intentions. One that I hope each of us will assume.

[1] As documented in *The Mayan Calendar and the Transformation of Consciousness* by Carl L. Calleman and Ian Xel Lungold's documentary "The Mayan Calendar Comes North."

True-Life Mystical Experiences in Egypt and Dendera With Hathor

—⟊⟊—

Lauren O. Thyme is obviously a person who knows her ancient Egypt profoundly. Her writing gives an almost hallucinatory impression of being there. Along the Nile is far and away the best novel about Ancient Egypt I have ever read. —Colin Wilson, world-famous author of The Outsider, From Atlantis to the Sphinx, The Occult, and many more.

I met Colin Wilson, a delightfully down-to-earth man, on my second of three metaphysical excursions to Egypt and we became acquainted. I'm amazed that he intuited my "hallucinatory impression of being there" when I later asked him to read my novel. Let me take you on an earlier tour, my first trip to Egypt, when *Along the Nile* was first impregnated into my mind.

During a meditation in 1996 I received a vision of an ancient Egyptian woman with a huge golden headdress who told me, "Go to Egypt. Go to Egypt. Go to Egypt." (Later I would find out her name was Hathor.)

I later met with a friend, Donna, who showed me exquisite photos of her recent trip to Egypt. When we got to photos of Dendera, I got excited. "Dendera? What is Dendera?" I asked her.

"It's a healing temple," Donna explained. "They also trained priestesses to be psychic and interpret dreams."

"I have to go to Dendera!" I announced. I didn't know why, but I always trust my gut feelings. Plus I had been a healer and psychic most of my life, so it somehow felt right.

I signed up for a metaphysical tour. Before I could actually go, a group of Islamic terrorists killed some tourists near Hetshepsut's Temple and the tour was cancelled. I researched online and only found one other tour that included Dendera—Quest Tours—and I signed up.

When I arrived in Giza at the fabulous 4-star Mena House Hotel overlooking the Pyramids, I met Quest Tours' owner, Mohammed Nazmy. We felt like instant friends and hugged with joy. Then he handed me an itinerary.

"Where's Dendera?" I exclaimed. "Aren't we going to Dendera?"

"No, Lauren, we had to cancel that portion of the trip. It requires an army convoy and we couldn't arrange it," Mohammed said sadly.

"But I have to go! It's why I joined your tour. Can I take a bus or train— or camel—or something?" I asked impetuously.

"I'm sorry," Mohammed explained. "It's an impossible journey on your own. Because of the danger of fundamental Islamists, tour regulations require an army convey to travel to that area."

I was beyond disappointed.

The next day our tour group visited the Great Pyramid complex. Impulsively I put my forehead (third eye) against a huge stone block low on the Great Pyramid. Suddenly I was in a vision: I was flying through stars in the cosmos. Suddenly I landed on Earth. I found myself in a dark, low, narrow enclosed walkway. It curved to the right. There was a tiny doorway with steps leading down.

I ran over to Mohammed to ask him what he thought it meant.

"That's Dendera," he said meaningfully.

"Oh, now I *really* need to go to Dendera!" I cried. "Are you sure there's no other way?"

Mohammed shook his head. "No, there isn't."

Several days later our group toured the Cairo Museum. In front is a large lotus pond with papyrus. I cried seeing it, not knowing why.

I wandered away from the group and found the King Tut exhibit. It was beautiful but didn't stir my emotions. Next to it was the Ancient Jewelry Exhibit. I went inside, looked at the jewelry and burst into tears again. I'm sure everyone must have thought I was crazy, crying over jewelry.

A few days later we flew south to Luxor. At dinner I saw our American tour guide whispering to Mohammed. I knew that meant we were going to Dendera. After dinner, Mohammed announced, "We are going to Dendera tomorrow!"

I suspected it was because of me and my vision. I ran over and hugged Mohammed in gratitude.

When we arrived at Dendera, I walked through the crumbling mud brick entrance and saw the Hathor columns of the Temple. Dendera was the home of Hathor, the golden woman I had first seen in my meditation, who had instructed me to "Go to Egypt." I fell down, prostrating myself on the dusty ground and cried some more. I was home!

The group went off with our assigned Egyptologist to view Dendera's Temple and grounds. I couldn't wait. I began running around the many acres, looking for my vision. Each time I stopped to gather my thoughts, an Egyptian man approached me. He was dressed in Western clothes so I knew he wasn't a Temple Guard, as they always wear a galabaya robe.

When I stopped, he would tell me, "You need to see the crypt."

I waved him away, saying, "No, thanks. I'm looking for something." I had been warned not to go off with Egyptian men, because they took "liberties" with Western women.

Then off I would go again, followed by the Egyptian man. I finally got discouraged and went to find Mohammed. He was up on the roof of the Temple. "Mohammed, where is my vision?" I asked him.

"I think it is over by the Sacred Lake," he replied, pointing to the now-dry lake enclosed with palm trees.

Off I went again, racing to the sacred lake, down some stairs, and looked into all the cubicles I saw there. Nothing. My vision was nowhere to be found.

The man came up to me again. "You need to see the crypt."

I was exhausted and frustrated. "Okay," I agreed. "Take me to the crypt."

We went into the massive Temple, with a forest of Hathor pillars all around. The strange man led me to a small, unadorned, dark room. He went over to a grate, lifted it up, turned on an electric switch and motioned to me. I was supposed to climb into a hole in the ground with a unknown Egyptian man? I decided to do it. He helped me down the ladder.

And there I was! In the middle of my vision. I walked along a dark, low, narrow enclosed walkway, which curved to the right. There was a tiny doorway with steps down—to the crypt!

We crawled through the doorway and made our way down to a beautiful limestone series of chambers, carved with absolutely elegant figures, designs, hieroglyphics, etc. I did a quick prayer for peace, a short meditation and took some pictures while the man stood quietly at my side.

When I was done, he asked, "Do you know what the crypt was used for?"

"No. I didn't even know there was a crypt here."

The man continued. "It was to store the sacred jewelry."

Sacred Jewelry!

Suddenly everything became clear. I had lived here before. I had taken care of, or at least knew about, the Sacred Jewelry.

He held out his hand for me to shake. "My name is Mohammed. I work for Mr. Nazmy in this part of his tour." Mohammed smiled. "I grew up in this area, in Qena, close to this temple. I used to play here all the time as a kid. Then I grew up and became an Egyptologist. I work for the Museum at Luxor. I don't usually talk to Mohammed's tour groups. I generally take care of details. But then I saw you get off the bus and I knew I had to take you to the crypt."

I was breathless with awe. The universe had gone through some amazing gymnastics to bring me to this moment.

Mohammed continued. "You're a Daughter of Hathor, aren't you?" He gazed at the 18K gold Hathor pendant necklace I was wearing, having bought it the day before in a Luxor jewelry shop.

"I'm not sure what you mean. But, yes, I think I am," I replied.

"You've lived here before."

"Yes, I think I have."

"I mean, before."

I understand what he meant. The young man was telling me he knew me in a previous life.

I then told him my whole story, including the vision I had at the Great Pyramid. "How did you know to bring me to the crypt?"

He shrugged. "I recognized you when you got off the bus. From…before…I knew you had to see the crypt."

My mind was in a whirl. No logical thoughts prevailed. Only an immense feeling of joy, a sense of homecoming, plus I was happy that I trusted my messages, visions, and intuitions. As if in a trance, I murmured, "I'm a writer. I'm going to write a book about this Temple someday."

Mohammed shyly added: "Many people have asked me to help them write their books about Dendera. I've always said no." He paused, and then continued. "But *you* I will help."

Not feeling like strangers any more, I hugged Mohammed from Qena.

When I returned to California, I tried valiantly to stay in touch with Mohammed from Qena who had taken me to the crypt. Phone calls were impossible then. Hardly anyone had cell phones. I called his mother's home, but no one spoke English there. Letters and packages disappeared into the void of a third world country postal department. I returned twice to Egypt, but Mohammed was out of the country both times. I never saw him again.

I wrote the book without him, but I acknowledge Mohammed from Qena as my spiritual guide to the Vision, which morphed into my book *Along the Nile* years later.

True-Life Mystical Experiences in Egypt and Karnak with Sekhmet

—◦∿◦—

Our metaphysical tour group was scheduled to go to Karnak, an immense temple complex covering many acres, built and added to over many centuries. A buzz went around our group when Mohammed Nazmy, owner of Quest Travel, announced that our group would be having a private showing inside the Ptah Sanctuary, including a famous statue of Sekhmet.

I confess to my almost-total ignorance at that time. Prior to this first trip I knew virtually nothing about Egypt, except perhaps the Giza complex with its pyramid and sphinx, Isis, Osiris, Ramses the Great, and Cleopatra. So when the name Sekhmet was announced, I shrugged at the excitement. Being from a mental Missouri—the Show Me state—I needed to be shown.

When we got to Karnak, I was overwhelmed by the immensity of the place. I could have easily gotten lost, so I stuck close to our group. And of course I didn't want to miss the private viewing of the popular Sekhmet.

It was late morning and the temperature was reaching 127°. I drank water non-stop and my legs were swollen from the heat, but I doggedly followed the others. Emil Shaker, our group's Egyptologist and resident comedian, led the way to the Sanctuary of Ptah. We had to wait for a prior group to finish their visit to the famous sanctuary, so we waited in whatever shade we could find.

Finally it was time to go inside. A quiver of excitement passed through me as we entered the tiny sanctuary. It was quite dark, lit only by a small opening in the ceiling to allow light into the room. The granite walls were bare of decoration. In the middle of the dining-room-sized space was the black basalt statue of the Neter Sekhmet. (Neter is the ancient Egyptian word for beings like Sekhmet, Isis, Anubis, Amun, and so on, which roughly translates to "energy source.")

Sekhmet, with her stylized Lioness head and larger-than-life-sized body of a woman, was positioned on a granite platform. Including the sun disk over her head, she stood well over seven feet tall. I had to look up to see her eyes. She was holding a carved ankh, the key of life, in one hand, placed at her side, and a Was scepter in the other.

To say she was commanding is an understatement. She took my breath away!

We had been advised throughout our travels in Egypt to avoid touching any of the antiquities, to maintain their condition for future visitors. Yet at this sanctuary we were not only allowed—but encouraged—to touch Sekhmet. Emil showed us the ritual of touching Her. Each of us was instructed to touch the top of Sekhmet's head, then our head. Then to touch Her heart and then our heart. Finally we were asked to move out of the way to allow the next person in line to do the same.

We lined up single file in front of her. When my turn came, I dutifully did as Emil had demonstrated. Her head, my head. Her heart, my heart. Then I stepped aside, to stand next to Her. I reached out to touch Sekhmet's arm. It was cool to the touch, especially after the blazing heat outside. I stroked it, amazed at both the coolness and smoothness of the basalt.

Suddenly, without warning, I felt the arm move under my hand. Then the statue turned and looked at me!

Her gaze was kindly, almost motherly, yet compelling. Involuntarily I screamed. Statues are not supposed to move! Then I ran outside.

I stood trembling in the courtyard of the sanctuary of Ptah, wondering if I had lost my senses, or was it the heat? Did I make it all up? Sekhmet's moving arm felt real beneath my hand and yet…

Several women from our group joined me outside. They were grinning at me.

One of them said, "That was amazing!"

"What was amazing?" I asked coyly, wanting verification, without exposing myself to ridicule.

"The statue. She turned and looked at you!"

"You saw it?" I could hardly believe her.

"Yes," the woman continued. "But that isn't all. The most amazing thing was when Sekhmet turned and looked at you, a *light* came out of her head and into your head."

"What?!" I exclaimed. "Oh, my goodness, what does this mean? Did she do that to you?" I asked her.

"No," the woman said sadly. "Just you."

The other woman nodded her head yes in agreement. I, alone, had been selected for the Neter's gaze, a metaphorical "tap on the shoulder."

I made a mental note that when I returned home I needed to research this Lion-headed being whose statue could move. Who is she? Why did she do that? What does she want from me?" I wouldn't have long to wait.

Meanwhile Emil, our tour group's Egyptologist, teased me incessantly during the rest of the tour about my being Sekhmet!

I had been back home from my metaphysical tour in Egypt for a week. I was dressed and standing in front of my mirror, applying make-up, preparing to go out. Unexpectedly Sekhmet appeared in the upper left corner of the mirror, looking as she had in Ptah's sanctuary, only alive now, not a statue.

"I have chosen you," she told me clearly, without introduction.

Then she continued. "I want you to return to Egypt as soon as possible, buy merchandise, and start a store."

I doubt anyone argues with Sekhmet, yet I couldn't help myself. "But... I'm a terrible salesperson and I can't run a business," I tried to explain to her.

"This is not about making money," Sekhmet continued undeterred. "I want you to bring Egypt to the People."

"Okay," I agreed reluctantly, assuming correctly she meant I was to buy ancient Egyptian reproductions to sell to interested people of the world. I would have been better off giving items away as I lost a lot of money in the seven years I ran The Egypt Store. Sekhmet was right in saying it wasn't about making money. But life with Sekhmet would turn out to be quite an adventure, worth every penny.

I consulted the internet for information about Sekhmet.

Everything I read about her was terrifying. Goddess of Wrath. Blood-thirsty. Ferocious. Avenger for her father Ra towards non-believers, drinking their blood in a frenzied rage, unable to stop murdering people until Thoth tricked her with red beer. Drunken Sekhmet then went to sleep and awoke as Hathor—so the legend goes. Where was the motherly Lioness who looked at me so gently and fondly in Egypt? And the Sekhmet in the mirror who gave me orders, but not in a frightening way, rather like a mother lion nudging her young cub in the direction she wanted it to go.

If you have already read the chapter, "Along the Nile: True-Life Mystical Experiences in Egypt and Dendera" you might be saying "Aha!" at this moment, because of the connections between Hathor and Sekhmet—and me. But that's the previous story.

I decided to trust my own experiences and intuitions (see the chapter, "The Importance of Psychic/Spiritual Discernment") with Sekhmet, rather than relying on what I read. I'm glad I did. The Sekhmet I know and love is not like the awful stories from the Internet. Nowadays, many people are having positive, albeit challenging, experiences with the Lioness Neter as well, so I feel vindicated. My coming years with Sekhmet would be an iteration of Lauren's Law #4: "Be aware. Transformation just ahead!"

I then contacted Mohammed Nazmy from Quest Travel, to find out when his next metaphysical tour was scheduled.

He was pleased to hear from me. "The next tour is a special one," he told me with excitement. "We are having a number of famous guest writers traveling with us, lecturing as well as conducting a symposium: John Anthony West, Robert Bauval, Graham Hancock, Robert Temple, Michael Baigent, and Colin Wilson. Dr. Zahi Hawass, curator of the Giza Plateau, will be leading the symposium."

I signed up at once and five months later I was back in the bosom of Mother Egypt.

Two miracles happened during this second tour:

1. Sekhmet told me to stand between the paws of the Great Sphinx at dawn in order to download information from the Book of Records. Mohammed took me to see Dr. Hawass to get permission. Because of that, our entire group got to experience dawn at the Sphinx.

2. I asked Mohammed if our tour could go to Abydos. I had written about the area in my new novel, *Along the Nile*, and needed to see it in person. I hadn't found any pictures of it, not even on the Internet. He explained the problem was the same as Dendera—we needed an army convey to get there and Abydos wasn't on our itinerary. But then, as the magician he is, Mohammed made sure to get us to Abydos. The cliffs and surrounding landscape looked exactly as I had described it in my novel, never having seen it in person.

Before I got to Egypt the second time, Sekhmet taught me "how to create." She informed me that she was primarily a Neter of Creation (not destruction), and that creation comes into being from the unformed universe through a combination of desire and passion, like the big bang. She taught me how to "hold the energy" so that my own creativity would be enhanced through temporarily withheld desire and passion. She told me that she had made me her High Priestess.

Through her tutelage I came to appreciate her enormous impact on another "selectee"—Ramses III (Ramses the Great). A number of carvings can be found with Sekhmet (often with her consort Ptah, also a creator/architect/master builder) bestowing energy and blessings on Pharaoh Ramses. Thus, rather than thinking of Ramses the Great as an egotistical maniac who couldn't stop building enormous projects, I began to see him in the light of being Chosen by Sekhmet, to build lasting monuments for us to discover thousands of years later.

I think I understand Ramses because the following seven years under Sekhmet's influence was a dizzying collage of creations:

- Meeting and becoming acquainted with wonderful people—Normandi Ellis (author of *Awakening Osiris* and others); Nicki Scully (author of *Shamanic Mysteries of Egypt,* and tour leader to Egypt); Karen Tate (author of *Sacred Places of Goddess*, founder of Isis Navigatum, radio show hostess, tour leader); Linda Iles; Lady Olivia Robertson (Archpriestess and founder of Fellowship of Isis); John Anthony West; Robert Bauval; Graham Hancock; Robert Temple; Colin Wilson; Loreon Vigne (owner/operator of the Isis Oasis); Charles and Joanne Elliott (Priest and Priestess, writers and poets); Vivianne Pulido (Charles and Vivianne also helped me run The Egypt Store); deTraci Regula (author of *The Mysteries of Isis*); and others too numerous to mention:

- Locating and buying merchandise from excellent local importers—and selling on the Internet at my new The Egypt Store website, at Psychic and Metaphysical Fairs, and on eBay (in its early days)

- Working on my novel *Along the Nile,* and writing numerous articles for my new Time Travel website

- Locating and listing 106 metaphysical tour groups with information about their tours (for free) on my Time Travel website
- Taking workshops and weekly classes with High Priest of Sekhmet, Peter Paddon (author of *Through the Veil* who was chosen by Sekhmet at the British Museum), and who subsequently ordained me as Priestess of Hathor
- Studying ancient Egypt intensely
- Lecturing and teaching on ancient Egypt in schools
- Establishing and consecrating my own Egyptian Temple/Iseum of Hathor, Sekhmet, and Anubis
- Performing weekly public rituals in my Temple/Iseum known as Becoming Rituals (Becoming Hathor, Becoming Sekhmet, etc.)
- Organizing and leading a third tour to Egypt and performing Becoming Rituals to each Neter at the Neter's home (Isis at Philae, Hathor at Dendera, Anubis in his chapel at Hetshepsut's Temple, and so on)

Then without warning, September 11, 2001 blasted the world into a new era. In 2002 the stock market crashed (this crash is not known to everyone), which wiped out most of my income. I moved in with Paul, my current partner, and closed my Temple/Iseum. No longer would I perform public rituals. Within a year I would close The Egypt Store and my two websites as well. The Egyptian chapter of my life ended. My novel *Along the Nile* would get published a few years later.

Sekhmet left, moving on to others whom she could guide and counsel in new creations. Peter Paddon explained this to me: Sekhmet disappears as suddenly as she arrives. Unlike other Neters like Hathor and Isis, you can't choose Sekhmet. She chooses you.

I feel blessed and honored to have been "chosen" by her and will never forget my life as her Priestess.

We Can Choose to Be Happy, No Matter What

—⁊⁊—

I have discovered all the things that we have been yearning for. It consists of three parts in order to have joy, peace and love:

Part 1—Here I refer to the Mayan Calendar of Consciousness. The Mayans reported "the top of the pyramid" as happening on October 28, 2011. On that date and forevermore we humans have ascended to the pinnacle of consciousness. It's called Conscious Co-Creation. That means we humans have now taken on the ability to consciously co-create with god, with the universe, to be as gods.

Part 2—The second part is that the Mind is no longer our ally. The main thing standing in the way of true peace and happiness is the Mind. (Shree Bhaghavan from Oneness Blessing says: "The mind is not mine. There are thoughts but no thinkers.")

Part 3—The final part is simply to be happy for everything on this planet, in myself, in yourself, no matter what it looks like to our mind. Be happy—positive, loving, forgiving, grateful—no matter what.

The Mind might see the Cabal or Illuminati or Bankers and say, "Bad Cabal. Bad Illuminati. Bad Bankers. The Cabal, the Illuminati, the Bankers have done/are doing bad things to me and the planet." And the mind will FOCUS on scientific, logical, even religious reasons, images, beliefs, facts to point to and say, "See. I'm right." The mind will go around and around in an endless loop of reasons, like a dog chasing its tail, creating proof, but not changing anything, while more of the same "bad" continues to be created.

The Mind might see the other political party and say, "Bad Party. The party has done/is doing bad things to me and the planet." And the mind FOCUSES on...etc., etc.

The Mind might see the rapist, the murderer, the criminal, the child molester, and say "Bad. This person has done/is doing bad things to me and the planet." And the mind FOCUSES on...etc.

The Mind might see severe weather, tornadoes, earthquakes, volcanic eruptions, oil or gas drilling, environmental degradation, deforestation, solar flares, reptilian ETs, or whatever, and say "Bad. This has done/is doing bad things to me and the planet." And the mind FOCUSES on...etc.

Now that we are Conscious Co-creators, the Mind can be dangerous to our health and well-being. The Mind has become our "Frankenstein's Monster."

We have outgrown the Mind. We can (and do) create anything. What gets created is what one focuses on. If one focuses on "bad," the "bad" gets all the creative energy of the universe, and so more of the same is created.

However, if one focuses on the positive—happiness, love, peace, harmony, forgiveness, gratitude, healing, etc.—then the positive gets all the creative juice, and so creates more of the same. Those same positive attributes then lead to positive solutions. This has always been true, but now it is true on a scale unparalleled in human history. Power that has been applied by the universe, starting with the Big Bang, is the power that is now gifted to human beings to utilize.

The Mind has difficulty in coming up with scientific, logical, religious reasons, images, beliefs, or facts to point to about "positive" and say, "See. I'm right," because the positive often doesn't make sense to the Mind. Positive attributes can be too ephemeral. No facts yet exist for the Mind to hook onto; the positive is not solid or manifested yet. The positive may actually be "counter-intuitive" to the mind.

For example, if I am molested by my father, and I practice, "I'm happy although he molested me. I'm grateful although he molested me. I forgive him for molesting me," the mind may refuse to listen, tell me I'm lying or crazy, turn away, dismissing me. BUT, if I *am* happy (even if I'm just "willing" to be happy) though I've been molested, I'm still happy. I'm happy as long as I'm happy. I can choose to be happy, no matter what. And then—because I am now a Conscious Co-Creator—happiness becomes my reality. (I've tried it and it works!) The molestation no longer has the energy or impact to continue to hurt me as it once did; it was me continuing to hurt me through my thoughts. I am released from bondage to create a new, happier world for myself. My ongoing suffering isn't necessarily based on what happens to me—but how I continue to think about it.

Another example: If a person is a Liberal and focuses on what the Conservatives are doing and calls it bad, judges it, focuses on it, obsesess on it, has demonstrations about it, gets angry and rants, the Liberal is actually helping to create more of the Conservative agenda. That means that the Conservative agenda gets twice the energy—both from itself and from the Liberal party. The way out for the Liberal is to exclusively focus on what he/she wants—and at the same time love, forgive, be grateful, and be happy about the Conservatives. And then, because the Liberal (and the Conservatives too, don't forget) is a Conscious Co-Creator, the positive solidifies and expands, the Liberal creates more of what is wanted in liberal solutions. (The Conservatives can do this in the same way.) The trick is that the Liberal must include the positive (love, forgiveness, gratitude, happiness) in order to make the essential shift to Enlightenment and Awakening, peace and harmony.

I have been hearing about "greedy bankers" or "greedy power brokers" over the last few years. Once I shift my attention from greedy, everything changes. (I had an epiphany about bankers and power brokers the other day, and now I love them—as people, as my family of souls on this planet. They can't stop wanting more and neither can most of us.)

"Greed" is in the collective consciousness at the moment, which is what can be changed. If I am a wealthy and powerful person, I want more money, possessions, and power. If I am a middle-class person, I want more money, possessions, and personal power. But money, possessions, and power are not what our consciousness is about anymore.

How much is enough? When does one become content with what one has? If one is happy and content, then one can be satisfied with what one has, no matter how much or how little. Are you beginning to see that we are all creating a reality together on this planet? Much of what we have been creating for a while is not for the health of humans, nature, animals, and the planet. We've been creating more of what we don't want, because that's what we've been focusing on. (I use "we" in the broad sense.)

Since October 28, 2011, we have been given the power to create a fabulous reality for everyone, starting with each of us doing our own work, becoming the best "me" each of us can be. It's not a matter of lecturing to "those out there" to fix the problems—but working with "me in here." As Gandhi said so eloquently, "Be the change you wish to see in the world." He meant it literally.

The ability to co-create is happening for the first time in history on a grand planetary scale. This is truly a time of ascension, freedom, creation—and we can take ourselves to heaven on earth NOW. We can choose it NOW.

We can choose to be happy, no matter what.

When Things Get Difficult, Stop!

L ately a series of incidents happened that reminded me that I need to stop when things get difficult. My goal is to remember this BE-FORE I go down certain avenues.

The modern catch phrase is: "When the going gets tough, the tough get going." Don't believe it!

What I recognize about myself, I've seen it in others, too.

If I'm sick, tired, overwhelmed, dehydrated, hungry, and/or pushing myself to finish a project and the project keeps tangling up, the message is —STOP!

I don't know how you operate, but often I'll say to myself, "just five more minutes, or I'll go one more step" but then problems arise or intensify. Since I write articles while using the computer and internet a lot, often the difficulty will be that my computer acts up, a program stops working properly, a program shuts down, an automated message keeps me from continuing, or an internet site shuts me out entirely. This might be a moment that someone will get upset with me. Sometimes I will get into such difficulty that I have to re-do a whole project from scratch. Recently it took me several additional weeks of grueling work to accomplish what I had set out to do—because I failed to stop and kept "shouldering too much work."

Therefore, I'm writing this article to remind myself. If it helps you, that's a bonus.

What I understand about life:
  —The universe and life are meant to be easy, enjoyable and even fun (Lauren's Law #3: "If it's easy, it's right")
  —The universe/nature/cosmic energy operates within cycles and rhythms
  — Timing is of the utmost importance (what doesn't work well right now will probably work out smoothly later on)
  —According to ancient Egyptians each hour of every day has its own unique energy
  —According to the ancient Mayans each day has its own unique energy
  —What works well one minute, hour, or day may not work well later and vice-versa
  —Fatigue, hunger, overwhelm, feeling inundated, etc. are messages that my body/mind uses to get my attention
  —Messages like fatigue, hunger, overwhelm, and feeling inundated tell me that energy is no longer flowing easily and to do something else
  —Creativity is not something I can turn on and off like a switch
  —Astrology/astronomy can alert me to appropriate timing, such as Mercury retrograde, full moons, eclipses, planetary transits, and so forth, that could affect what I'm doing
  —Psychic and spiritual discernment is critical to my well-being and thus my work
  —Psychic messages may be telling me that I'm taking a wrong turn and to stop and reevaluate before continuing
  —Impatience, pushing myself beyond my limits, and trying to cut corners are not helpful and in fact often create more problems
  —The logical mind isn't any help in determining what to do or not to

do under these circumstances and can even contribute to further problems.

I'm sure this is just a partial list. You could probably add more to it from your own experiences.

What have I learned?

When things get difficult, STOP!

If I try to push the river, the river pushes back.

Slow down. I don't have to hurry.

Take time to review the flow of energy both within and outside my body.

Listen and take appropriate action from any messages I get.

Relax and do something I enjoy for a while. Rest. Eat. Play.

Don't continue the project unless and until I get a green light.

Eventually..... the task will get done. If I wait for the right time, the task will get done easily and effortlessly.

Remember and pay attention—because I already know these admonitions!

In the meantime, when running into difficulties, STOP.

Lauren's Laws

These "LAWS" are based on a lifetime of observation, learning, experimenting, trial and error. You don't have to "believe" in any of them. The Laws are presented here for contemplation.

1. We each live in our own separate universe. Everything in that universe is true and correct for that universe. There is no truth with a capital T, no reality with a capital R.

2. Love is the building block of the universe, from which everything emanates. It's in you, around you, it IS you. If you cannot feel love right now, don't worry. It's still there.

3. If it's easy, it's right. If a project is or becomes difficult, stop. You might be going the wrong direction, using the wrong tools, being in the wrong time or place, beating your head against a brick wall. Wait for clarity. (Refer to the previous chapter, "When Things Are Difficult,
Stop!)

4. Be aware. Transformation is just ahead.

5. $M = ET^2$ Miracles/Matter/Time Equals Energized Thought

Squared...(of Two or more people)

Miracles of physical matter, events, space, or time can be speeded up, increased, or transformed through the elevated (spiritual) interaction of two or more people. One person plus one person equals more than two people. Two people plus two people equals MUCH more than four people. The increase of energy is exponential.

6. I can unconditionally love someone, but do not have to go to dinner with him or her.

7. A relationship lasts as long as it lasts—not one minute longer. And you'll know the moment the relationship has ended.

8. When a relationship comes to an end, bless it and move on. There's no turning back once that lesson is learned.

9. Relationships are like buses—there's always the next one to catch to take you to a new destination.

10. When a difficult person arrives in your life, love that person, forgive, and be grateful. The universe has sent that person to you as a gift for your learning.

11. When a difficult situation arrives in your life, love that situation, forgive, and be grateful. The universe has sent that situation to you as a gift for your learning.

12. When you need something, give.

13. The universe is all about timing. So is everything in your life.

14. There's no one to blame.

15. Ended relationships are not failures. Once you are finished learning with a person, you are on to the next (it might be yourself) for the purpose of personal learning, growing and evolving.

16. Instant Karma. Karma can be quick depending on your awareness, for the purpose of instant learning. The more you learn, the more aware you become, the faster karma works. It is a self-reinforcing loop.

17. Grace trumps karma.

18. Tell the truth…as fast as you can. This may not mean immediately. Sometimes appropriate timing is involved. Truth opens up all kinds of avenues that may not have been open before.

19. There is no such thing as a lie, not even a "little white lie." This includes telling outright falsehoods as well as failing to tell the truth. Lies cannot and do not exist. Everyone is psychic. Everyone intuits another's emotions and intentions and behaves according to that intuition, even if the intuition is unconscious. Attempting to lie (or failing to tell the truth) will create problems for everyone including oneself. Many of today's world problems are based on attempts to lie. Many movies are based on the interaction around a falsehood. That kind of movie plot couldn't exist without an attempt to conceal, hide, avoid, or run from the truth; the movie would be over in a matter of minutes had the truth been told at the beginning.

20. Everything is connected to everything as though by an immense Spider Web of Life. A change will vibrate the entire web; thus ONE person CAN make a difference. (Quantum physicists and string theorists seem to be in agreement with me.)

21. Everything is perfect, no matter what it looks like, for the purpose of growing, learning, and evolving.

22. Everything is perfect, no matter whether it changes or not.

23. Forgiveness is selfish—for your own peace, happiness, and well-being.

24. Pay attention as if your life depends on it. It does.

25. Everyone is psychic.

26. As I transform myself, others transform themselves in my presence.

27. The mind is not my friend.

28. Grief helps me know how much I love someone.

Miracles and My New Gold Life

I love to share stories with you—to encourage you to be open to even greater miracles than you already have known, or, if you haven't had any, to be willing to receive lots of miracles from the universe. I also share my stories so you know that miracles can and do happen all the time. I'm eager for them to happen to you! I'm not saying that life is necessarily easy all the time—yet. However, you can become a recipient of a miraculous life.

My own life is half miraculous and half hard as the dickens. Often it depends on the day or time I check in! Yet, no matter how difficult the other half is, I wouldn't give up the miraculous part of my life for any amount of money or health. Since I've been quite sick for thirty-nine years, that's a lot to say.

Miracles don't have gradations, nor are there levels of difficulty. Miracles don't come in shapes or sizes or amounts, although my logical/rational partner, Paul, might have disagreed with this. To me there are only just—MIRACLES. A miracle either happens—or it doesn't.

A miracle could consist of getting something in the mail you were already expecting—and yet happy to receive.

A miracle might be getting help changing a flat tire, a neighbor dropping by to give you flowers, or a business not charging you for something you expected to pay for. (Yes, these miracles do happen.)

A miracle can be putting a tiny seed in the ground and sometime later eating its harvest.

A miracle can be a fertile egg being sat upon endlessly by a gleaming red hen, which weeks later becomes a fluffy yellow chick.

And a miracle can be life-altering.

When receiving a miracle, I simply say to the universe —THANK YOU! (sometimes over and over again) Gratitude seems to be part of a function that helps to create miracles.

The other part of the function is to ASK. "Ask and ye shall receive." You can read the two chapters that help with the asking part: "The Universal Bank Account" and "How to Easily Get What You Want."

I'm going to talk about a life-altering miracle I received in 1995. I'm not bragging or saying I'm special, because I'm not. I'm ordinary. I'm simply sharing this miracle with you so that you KNOW you could get a life-changing miracle, too. Here's my story.

I had been bedridden for months with chronic fatigue syndrome and fibromyalgia. I slept 16-18 hours a day. I was often in pain and depressed. Paul did all the chores, cared for me, and paid the bills. Often I was too sick and exhausted to even brush my teeth.

One day I felt that I had enough of suffering. I sat up in bed and yelled at God. Yes, *yelled!* "Either take me home right now…or do something else!" Then I fell back into bed, miserable and unhappy.

At that time I was into my third year of trying to qualify for Social Security disability. I finally hired an attorney, who informed me that two specialists he knew had a 100% approval rating for their clients to receive disability for the same illness I had. The only drawback was it would cost $6,000 to get all the tests required from those specialists. I had already spent $150,000 over the course of twenty years, trying to get well.

My partner Paul asked me to call my Dad to solicit that money to help with my doctor expenses, in order to approve my disability. "Your father can take it out of your inheritance," Paul explained calmly.

I had never asked for anything from my Dad before. He and I had a terrible relationship stemming back to my early childhood and I stayed away from him as much as possible. Now I was being asked to call and request him to help me. Reluctantly I did so.

I explained the situation. I needed $6,000 for specialists, who would then advise Social Security how sick I was. I further remarked that he could take the money out of my inheritance.

The only reply from my Dad was, "I can't."

I asked again, this time feeling really shaky.

"I can't," was again his answer.

"Please, Dad," I added, now beginning to cry. "I need your help. This is for my life. Why can't you? Tell me why."

"I just can't" he said again and hung up the phone.

I went outside to my garden and sobbed. This refusal felt like a stab to the chest.

I heard the soothing voices of my Elders speaking to me. "Be grateful," they told me.

"Okay," I replied. "I'm grateful for Paul. I'm grateful for this house. I'm grateful for this garden. I'm grateful for my children and my friends."

The Elders spoke again. "You forgot your Dad."

I gulped. How on earth could I be grateful for *him?* When he had molested me and hurt me and now refused to help me when I was so desperate and had nowhere to turn? I took a deep breath.

I trust my Elders. They wouldn't ask me to do this without a good reason. I decided to try it. "I'm grateful for my father. I'm grateful he molested me!" Suddenly, inexplicably, I was awash with emotion. I *was* grateful. Then I cried all the harder.

In the next few weeks my health began to improve. Paul gave me the

$6,000 for the doctors. They performed the necessary tests and I eventually submitted all the documentation to Social Security.

A few weeks later my sister Dale called to tell me that Dad was in the hospital. His prostate cancer, which we thought had been cured, had returned, and now cancer had metastasized throughout his whole body, including his brain. He couldn't vocalize well, although he could understand what was said to him. Dale asked me if I would make arrangements for Dad to go into a nursing home, since she worked and I didn't. I agreed to do so. I stayed at his house for two weeks, making sure that he was comfortable and cared for at the nursing home. I drove his girlfriend to see him whenever she wanted, often several times a day.

Dad mostly slept. He never thanked me for my efforts. Never told me he loved me. Yet somehow I was no longer upset with him. I felt quite at peace. In fact, I prayed that he wouldn't experience pain and suffering. He didn't.

I went home for a rest, accidentally broke my foot, and wasn't able to return. Dale went for a few days, then she went home.

Two weeks later the nursing home called to tell me Dad had died. I didn't cry. I was relieved.

Five months went by. Dale was pregnant and almost due to deliver her baby.

Subtly at first, then stronger and stronger, I kept getting a feeling. Something *big* was coming my way. When I told Paul about my message, he asked: "Are you going to win the lottery?"

"No," I replied, "but it's enormous. I just don't know what. I guess we'll see in time."

Meanwhile my sister Dale delivered her baby, Jackson, and we made arrangements to go see her by the end of the week.

A couple of nights later, around midnight, I was awakened by the Elders and asked to go to my computer. Often they ask me to write things, but never in the middle of the night before. Dutifully, however, I went to my computer and waited for their words.

Here is the poem they dictated:

> *Twirling with the wind we are the leaves of the universe*
> *Victorious in our freedom*
> *Divine*
> *Yet hesitant, we deny our dance and with measured beat*
> *cling to desolation, lovelessness and loss*
> *Anonymous and hollow, hoping for an echo of clarity, we*
> *interrogate the silent void.*
> *A distant melody, faint but clear, reverberates: "Sing to*
> *me. Answers will frolic like questions, and doubts will*
> *evaporate like poetry in sunlight. When you choose life,*
> *life chooses you. A golden rainbow will come, a shower,*
> *washing clean your fears. Lay down your burdens and re-*
> *joice."*
> *Phrases hang in the wind like yesterday's laundry, brows*
> *furrow in soil fecund with imagination, while lips form*
> *words unwittingly. "Who? We ask, like awakening owls—*
> *who?"*
> *"All of you," the universe replies*
> *"What?"*
> *"A golden life."*
> *"Why?"*
> *"Because it is time."*
> *"When?"*
> *"Now."*

I then printed out the poem, left it on my desk, and returned to bed.

In the morning I showed the poem to Paul. "This isn't your best work," he pronounced, like the good English professor that he is.

Later that day we drove to my sister Dale's house, to visit her and her new baby Jackson. I kept thinking about the poem. I couldn't get it out of my mind. What did it mean? Why did the Elders wake me up in order to have me type it?

Paul and I had a nice time with my sister, the new baby, and her family, then drove the hour's distance home. Again I kept thinking about the poem. I mentioned it to Paul. "I don't understand the poem. What does it mean?"

He shrugged in reply. Then he said, "Why don't we go out to your favorite restaurant tonight?"

I was happy since I was exhausted by the trip and the visit. When we got home, I laid down to rest for dinner. Paul joined me on the other side of the bed.

I was again musing about the poem. All of a sudden I realized that it wasn't a poem at all.

It was a *telegram!*

A new gold life! I got up and retrieved the poem from my desk, lay down on the bed and reread it.

Without warning, the ceiling of our bedroom "flew" open and gold light streamed into my body from above.

I'm used to unusual experiences, so I just lay back and let it flow into me.

I could feel the gold light in my blood, my brain, the cells of my body, even in my personality. The gold light continued to surge through me for about thirty minutes.

Just as quickly as it began, the gold light stream stopped. I felt different, giddy, light-headed, and happy.

Then I heard the Voice of the Elders. "Look at your watch."

I did. It was 6:18 p.m. on October 27, 1995.

"This is your new birthday. Don't ever celebrate your old birthday ever again."

"I will do as you say," I replied.

Then I got up and went to my computer. I have an astrology program on it and within minutes I was looking at my new birth chart. I had changed from a Capricorn to a Scorpio.

I had always wanted to be a Scorpio. I resonated with the intensity, passion, and emotionality of that sign. Not only that, but my former chart was very difficult, while the new one was much easier to live with.

So much changed. It took about a year for Paul and me to get used to my new self. Instead of holding things back, I now blurted out what I felt—thanks to Moon in Sagittarius, coupled with the intensity of Sun in Scorpio. My psychic abilities got stronger than ever. My health significantly improved for the next five years. The most stunning alteration (due to Jupiter and Moon in Sagittarius and a few other astrological aspects) was my desire to travel, plus writing and publishing. I had never before liked to travel, preferring to stay home and garden. Suddenly I wanted to travel everywhere, internationally too, especially to sacred sites and did so for the next few years. I wrote articles about my travels and spirituality, along with books.

After visiting Egypt, I studied the Egyptian Mystery School, was ordained as a Priestess of Hathor, and transformed my apartment into an Egyptian Temple. With the help of Paul's grandson Corey I created two websites and started an online store. When I compare the two Laurens, I'm amazed at the differences.

There were two more changes.

I was approved for Social Security disability *and* received my inheritance, both just a few months after my Dad died.

One could say all this is a miracle—and I'd have to agree. And who knows? Maybe my demanding (asking for help from God and the universe) and gratitude towards my father were part of the creation of the miracle. I don't know anything for certain. But I do find all this interesting and hopeful, don't you?

If This Is Not My Body,
Then Whose Body Is It?

—ʍ—

The body is not mine," say many Buddhists, as does Shree Bhagavan, from the Oneness Blessing University in India. Whose body is this then? Before I answer that, I'm going to delve into a few other areas of speculation.

I've noticed that very successful people seem to have one thing in common—a *lot* of energy. Often they may not need much sleep, only four or five hours, and the rest of the time they operate like human dynamos. With little or no sleep or rest, they perform beautifully for decades. This ability seems to be built into their bodies. They don't necessarily seem to do anything to deserve it. (Of course, they might have training, talent, luck, breaks, family, and connections, too, but I'm focusing on the physical aspects at this time.)

I've noticed that many people find it easy to do what they want with their bodies. When a person is healthy, it is easy to believe that they are in charge of the body. Oftentimes when asking the body to accomplish something we want, it gets done. Except for short detours into flu and colds, broken bones or torn ligaments, the body miraculously and quickly stabilizes and heals itself—seemingly according to our wishes. But this is just an illusion. The body is in charge, not us.

When a person gets a chronic illness, is aging rapidly, or developing cancer, all bets are off. Any of these problems makes us notice that the body is not cooperating with our desires.

I suddenly got ill with chronic fatigue syndrome and fibromyalgia thirty-nine years ago. I found out the body didn't belong to me and I had little control over it. Most of the time I cannot make the body do what I want it to do. I say *the* body, because it isn't *my* body. (e.g., I cannot go to sleep or wake up when I want to, without severe consequences like headaches, nausea, dizziness, grumpiness, brain fog, swollen glands, or more fatigue than usual.) Before I became disabled and was still working, I was usually late to work every morning. I could be punctual any other time of the day; the problem was just mornings. I had a fight on my hands every morning, because the body didn't want to get up when I wanted it to arise. Setting the alarm clock didn't help. I'd turn off the alarm or ignore the radio and instantly fall back asleep, no matter how much effort I put into waking. I believe these symptoms were already showing a tendency toward thyroid problems, chronic fatigue/fibromyalgia, and hypothalamus-pituitary-adrenal axis problems.

This body does what it wants to do, regardless of what I desire. I'm not in the driver's seat—I'm on the passenger's side, without an airbag, automatic windows, reclining seats, brakes or accelerator, heater, air conditioner, or even a door handle. Sometimes the radio works, sometimes not. I've been on a bumpy ride in this physical vehicle for decades and it shows.

I often say that my mind draws up a contract which my body cannot pay. For example, I make a plan to go to an appointment, but the body is often not able to follow through physically with my plan and I'm forced to cancel. Thus I have a saying: "The mind makes a contract which the body cannot pay."

Many people in today's world are sick and tired. Since 1974 we've had a huge increase in chronic fatigue syndrome and fibromyalgia, cancer now affects 25% of the world's population, while vascular diseases and diabetes are on the upswing. Some medical authorities say vascular and diabetic problems are due to how we eat, as well as lack of exercise. What about the other problems? They seem more mysterious.

My partner Paul, who weighed a mere 158 pounds most of his life, had normal blood pressure and excellent cholesterol levels, and had always been "healthy as a horse." In 2012 he had a heart attack and stents were inserted into an artery. He's an English professor, never did vigorous exercise and eats what he wants. He's 88 years old. He says his health isn't due to his character—it's in his genes. Who knows? Why is Paul so lucky?

I've found a number of theories that explain the variance in bodies. Remember, I'm not a trained scientist, although I study scientific inquiry, notice, and contemplate a lot.

First let's look at genes. My twenty-nine year-old step-grandson came down with a mysterious illness. He said the severity of his problems is high so he was pretty sick. Recently he had his DNA tested. His DNA showed that his body has a moderate inclination towards inflammatory diseases, as well as potential problems with his thyroid and adrenals. He's a young person, in the prime of his life and career. Why him? Why now? Why ever?

Dr. Bruce Lipton, author of *The Biology of Belief*, a former medical school professor and research scientist, says (along with many other scientists) that it's not only our DNA affecting us. There are switches that turn DNA off and on. These switches are controlled by our environment.

"His experiments, and that of other leading edge scientists, have examined in great detail the processes by which cells receive information. The implications of this research radically change our understanding of life. It shows that genes and DNA do not control our biology; that instead DNA is controlled by signals from outside the cell, including the energetic messages emanating from our positive and negative thoughts. Dr. Lipton's profoundly hopeful synthesis of the latest and best research in cell biology and quantum physics is being hailed as a major breakthrough showing that our bodies can be changed as we re-train our thinking." —*http://www.thetruthabout-foodandhealth.com/healtharticles/biology-of-belief-bruce-lipton-genes-cell.html*

Dr. Lipton's friend, Rob Williams, posits in his workshop, Psych-K, that it's not just any thinking that we must retrain. Conscious thoughts only make up about five percent of our consciousness. Therefore, a human being must somehow connect and communicate with, and subsequently change the remaining 95% of subconscious thoughts in order to make significant changes. —*https://www.psych-k.com/*

Furthermore, Dr. Candace Pert in her book *Everything you Need to Know to Feel Go(o)d,* has come up with yet another radical theory. Dr. Pert is not an airy-fairy New Ager. Her website biography states:

"Dr. Candace Pert is an internationally recognized pharmacologist who has published over 250 scientific articles. She received her Ph.D. in pharmacology from Johns Hopkins University School of Medicine, served as Chief of the Section on Brain Biochemistry of the Clinical Neuroscience Branch of the National Institute of Mental Health (NIMH), held a Research Professorship in the Department of Physiology and Biophysics at Georgetown University School of Medicine in Washington, DC, and is currently working in a private company developing an AIDS vaccine in addition to treatments for other diseases." —*http://candacepert.com/*

Her concept: the subconscious mind does not reside in the body. The subconscious mind IS the body. The body is the subconscious mind.

Dr. Michael Newton, during his forty years as therapist, hypnotherapist, and teacher, uncovered the mystery of life through working with thousands of patients. His findings: in our sojourn during our "Life between Lives" in the so-called spiritual realm, we each decide what we need to learn and with whom, make a contract for our new life, and immerse ourselves in that life at conception. Then the plan begins to unfold. When the body gets to the end of its tenure by accident or illness, it dies—while our authentic self continues into the spirit realm, and ultimately goes to live in yet another body.

That means what happens to each of us in life is not a "crap-shoot" as my partner Paul so eloquently explained. Our lives are exquisitely thought out and planned in advance, including what happens to our physical bodies. The problem might be that we don't remember what we planned. Hence, we may feel shocked when the body doesn't do what we expect it to do. Patients have gone to Dr. Newton in their "search for meaning, purpose, and a divine plan in their lives." And probably looking for answers to their problems, physical, and otherwise.

Robert Schwartz, author of *Your Soul's Plan: Discovering the Real Meaning of the Life You Planned Before You Were Born*, proposes a rationale for life's difficulties and a way to appreciate and resolve them. Mr. Schwartz offers stories of ten individuals who planned their lives to include huge challenges, meant to foster growth, healing of unwanted patterns, and evolution of their spiritual beings.

Lastly, I want to mention astrology. Although astrology has gotten a bad rap from some scientists and religions, after studying it for forty-three years, I find it abounds with vital information (natal, progressed, comparative, and astro-cartography charts) and helpful timing tips to know when our DNA switches are in position to be activated (transits). Like DNA, astrology shows tendencies and predispositions, not just for our physical bodies but also for behavior, personality traits, and relationships. Astrology is like a personal (possible) road map of our journey through life.

Back to my main question…whose body is this? Apparently it is a vehicle on loan to us from the universe, with a consciousness and intelligence of its own, one that can digest, assimilate, excrete, and run its multiple functions without our conscious knowledge or assistance. The body is attached to all the goodies (DNA proclivities, plans for experiences and people, environmental receptors, and a blueprint to follow) in order for us to learn, grow, and develop further into spiritual beings. The body is a living tool, an organic apparatus for us to live in, while we practice what we came here to experience.

I had a silly metaphor pop into my head—a body is like various cars. When we're young and vibrant, many of us are driving fast, sporty cars. If we're older or ill, we may have an old clunker, maybe public transportation, or simply walk. When mature or wiser, we might opt for an economical or hybrid car. As we age, we may get too old, ill, or blind to drive anymore and our license to drive is taken away. I've noticed some people can make changes to their "cars" through exercise, organic food, clean water, positive thoughts. But can these environmental influences alter the basic structure of our beings? Can the body modulate, but not actually heal, unless healing is the plan? What about me? I've tried so much and am still sick. The answer is that I don't know.

However, I'm not saying we should sit back and give up if we are being physically, mentally, psychologically, or age challenged.

After much studying and doing past life readings for decades, I have a hunch that if we don't learn, we come back and try the lesson again. The same may be true of those who commit suicide. However, the next time the challenges might be even tougher.

One thing I have realized in all my studies and visits to doctors is that bodies are not mechanical. We cannot take them apart and put them back together like machines. We are not given medicine to heal our bodies, but generally to mask existing symptoms. Surgery has its limits, too. Bodies operate synergistically, collaboratively, and cooperatively within themselves—organically.

So—what about me and this body? I believe I set up this body to operate in exactly the way it does. I tried hundreds of allopathic doctors, not to mention decades of alternative healing modalities. So much so that I wrote a book about my learning: *Alternatives for Everyone: A Guide to Non-Traditional Health Care.* Nowadays I find that surrender, trust, and gratitude work best for me. And I continue to improve my core being.

Regarding my grandson and Paul—and the rest of us. There's no one and nothing to blame *or* applaud. What goes on in our bodies is wonderfully planned and amazingly executed—presumably by our higher selves. "Everything is perfect," my Elder friends tell me, "for our learning, growth, and evolution."

Gratitude

—∞—

I'm a meta-scientist, which means that I'm always on the lookout for some new and improved way to live spiritually within the universe. One of the pieces of Universal Wisdom I have learned was gratitude, which I practiced for many years. Whenever something wonderful, large or small, occurs, I always remember to say "Thank you."

But in early 1998, I began to have an inkling that there was something more, a higher octave of gratitude. I needed to practice being grateful for the unpleasant things, too. I had already become aware that "everything is perfect" in the Universe, no matter what it looks like. Therefore, each lesson or challenge, regardless of its appearance, was a precious gift for my growth and evolution and linked to the Collective Consciousness as well. So I started to practice a new form of gratitude—being grateful even if the "negative something" never changed.

I came down with the flu for a week or two and decided it was a good place to begin. I began saying both out loud and in my head, "Thank you for this flu. I'm very grateful for being sick. I'm thankful that I can't get out of bed, have a fever, aches and pains, etc." At first it was only an exercise. Every time I said I was thankful, my conscious mind responded adversely.

"Are you crazy? How can you be grateful for this? It doesn't make any sense." But I doggedly persisted, ignoring my mind, feeling that somehow what I was doing was right.

The first thing I noticed was that my mind slowly stopped protesting. A sense of peace and calm replaced my mind's antagonism. I didn't seem to care so much that I was sick in bed. In fact, I began to feel happy and content although I was still sick. "Hmmm," I thought to myself. "This is interesting." I even encouraged Paul to practice, too. Instead of telling me how upset he was that I was sick, I asked him to say instead, "I'm really thankful you're sick." I'm sure he thought I had lost a few of my marbles.

Our car broke down and I continued to practice gratitude. "Oh, thank you so much for our car breaking down. I'm grateful we have to spend money to fix our car." And so on. Whatever unpleasant, unfortunate, or upsetting event occurred, I countered with "I'm grateful," knowing that even if I didn't understand why the event was happening, it was somehow perfect. Calmness, peace, and happiness continued to grow each time I practiced.

I began to look at other things. For example, I had put on quite a bit of weight in the last few years. I practiced being grateful for my weight. I practiced gratitude for money problems. In short, I started being grateful for everything I could think of. Serenity and joy flooded my consciousness. I found this shift to be quite fascinating and thought I was doing quite well with my newfound practice.

However, the Universe, in its wisdom, helped me deepen my resolve. On the fourth day of a three-month trip to Europe, I fell and badly sprained my right arm (I'm right handed). Not only were we unable to travel because of the pain, but I also couldn't move my arm, couldn't dress myself, had difficulty feeding myself, and washing my hair. In short, I was severely hampered. So I practiced gratitude. Although I was somewhat bored sitting in a small Italian hotel room with only CNN for entertainment, I wasn't upset. I found that being grateful precluded anger, depression, and other unpleasant emotions. (Thank you for my boredom!) My arm healed rapidly, which is unusual for me, and we began to travel again.

When I returned home from my trip, I broke my toe. Immediately I became thankful for my broken toe and forgot all about it. In three days it had mended tremendously and in less than two weeks had completely healed.

I discerned that I had "stumbled" onto something powerful. Being grateful for what has been termed negative events means to fully embrace all of my life. Embracing all things in my life meant that I had moved from passive acceptance into active gratitude. In a sense, I was taking charge of my life and embracing responsibility for all things within it, which seemed to change my whole attitude towards negativity.

I turned my attention outward and began to practice gratitude for many things that exist on our planet—pollution, war, hunger, violence, and so forth. My attitude towards those situations shifted dramatically as well. I'm not saying that I sit back and do nothing about negative situations. I do what I can and am led to do. However, in the meantime, I have a different and spiritual perspective on personal and world situations, which brings me contentment and joy in my outlook and attitude.

People say they want peace and harmony in life. I've realized that peace and harmony are a state of mind, an attitude, rather than being linked to a pleasant event, situation, or condition. That state of mind can be achieved through gratitude. Unfortunate, unpleasant and inharmonious events and situations can and probably will continue to happen in life, but with gratitude the focus shifts from unhappiness and despair to serenity, harmony, and happiness.

In a Coma With Ginny

—ɯɯ—

I n a life filled with odd and novel psychic/spiritual experiences, my week with Ginny ranks among the oddest.

April 26, 2012

I called my friend Barb. She was upset and crying, as her only sister Ginny had a heart attack the day before, while she was visiting friends in Boston. Apparently Ginny had been sleeping next to her partner John. He woke to hear unsettling gurgling noises in the night. He discovered Ginny wasn't breathing. John started CPR on Ginny immediately and called for the paramedics. Ginny was subsequently rushed into intensive care and put on a respirator, along with being hooked up to IV's, machines, and medications. The diagnosis was cardiac arrest.

April 27

The day after talking with Barb another friend of mine, Huddie, called me. I mentioned Ginny in our conversation. Huddie impetuously said "Let's try to help Ginny." As a psychic I have experienced many unusual encounters, including miraculous healings, so I was eager to try. Huddie believed that Ginny would have a good recovery, but I wasn't so sure. I tuned into Ginny and could feel her physical status. I intuited that she had brain damage and was comatose.

At that moment I could hear Ginny talking to me telepathically. Her body was in a coma in Boston, but her spirit was very much alive. She instructed me to tell her partner John and her daughter Anna that she needed them to talk to her non-stop. She wanted John to tell jokes and Anna to sing songs. Ginny also asked for both of them to stroke her temples while joking and singing. In retrospect I believe her request was an attempt to heal the damage that had occurred in her brain's frontal lobes.

I called my friend Barb immediately to tell her what I was doing and also about the transaction between Ginny and me. Barb has consulted with me for years, receiving psychic and spiritual counseling. In those sessions I received and imparted correct information about her, her family, and pets, so she was amenable to my report. I told Barb about the stroking of the temples.

When I got off the phone, Ginny popped into my room to let me know I had forgotten to impart a piece of her message. I sent the following email to Barb:

Email April 27
"Hi. Ginny reminded me—I forgot [she wants] John to tell her jokes, all his jokes. She also wants Anna to sing to her. I pray she will recover soon and completely. Keep me posted. Lauren"

Barb then called John on his cell phone in Boston and gave him the instructions from Ginny via me. John and Anna then did as instructed. Some hours later John called Barb to tell her that Ginny was responding to the stroking, jokes, and songs. Although she wasn't conscious or talking yet, Ginny was making sounds and flickering her eyelids and trying to open her eyes. Her progress was encouraging to everyone, including the doctors.

For the next few days, Barb and I stayed in touch via her cell phone, to receive and relay information from Ginny's spirit—talking to me in Washington state—to her partner, John, still in Boston.

April 28   5 a.m.

I'm awakened as Ginny roused me. "They are doing something to me! What are they doing? I don't understand."

"I don't know," I told Ginny. Then I had a "discussion" with her about her health. I told her that when she recovered, she would need to cut back on her rigorous business and personal schedule and devote more time to taking care of herself.

"I don't want to die," she said to me. "Am I going to die—or will I get better?"

"I'm not sure, Ginny," I replied.

Barb confirmed later that Ginny always pushed herself and demanded her body to do her bidding. Now, however, Ginny's body wasn't responding to those demands. As it was too early in the morning, I told Ginny I would call Barb later and find out what the doctors were doing. I took the opportunity to encourage Ginny's spirit to relax and surrender to the spirit realm, which would bring her peace. She left without comment.

I was getting used to Ginny brusquely coming and going. Later that morning Barb told me the doctors had been performing brain scans on Ginny to determine brain activity. They discovered that Ginny was having seizures and they started her on anti-seizure medication. Her short-lived progress deteriorated rapidly after that.

Same day—April 28   5 p.m.

Ginny appeared to me, even more agitated. "I'm all alone. They want to pull the plug!" Apparently John and Anna had gone home exhausted when visiting hours were over, to have some dinner, relax, and hopefully rest. The tests had shown extensive brain damage and the doctor was advising John to discontinue Ginny's life support. Ginny was hearing and reacting to all this, helpless to do anything except contact me. Ginny, according to her sister Barb, was not comfortable with helplessness. I said some soothing words, but Ginny's spirit didn't stick around to listen.

April 28 My email to Barb

"Dear Barb—Ginny has come to see me twice today, but I was feeling so sick, I had to go to bed. Just up now at 8 p.m. So finally I get to write to you.

The first time Ginny came to see me she was very upset. She asked me about the tests that were being done, the seizures, etc. and I told her what I knew from your email. She asked if she would continue to have seizures the rest of her life and if she would have brain damage. I told her I didn't know. I asked my Elders for an update, but got no response. Their lack of response doesn't mean anything one way or another, I've discovered. Her health is something that the doctors need to discuss."

I told her I have asked for a miracle, but I can't guarantee one. It depends on what Ginny's higher self and the universe have decided. I told Ginny to practice feeling "the universe" around her when she's out of her body—to be relaxed and comforted."

Then she left."

The second time she came back was about 5 p.m. my time (she woke me up from a nap and I looked at my watch) so that was about 8 p.m. Boston time. She was even more upset and said she felt all alone, abandoned. Did John and Anna leave or go home? She also was frantic about "don't pull the plug!" Yet she said she couldn't face having more physical problems than she already does. So she needs to "talk" to all of you—to discuss what might be the best course of action. And she also felt that perhaps you all should wait until all tests are in and the docs can tell you what they conclude—and then try to make the best decision."

Just now I asked for her to talk to me but nothing is happening. I think she comes when she feels she needs to talk to me."

So—I'm sorry to burst your bubble. Your earlier email sounded really upbeat. But I have to report what is real, as far as I'm picking it up. At least that way you know she is talking to you, and she knows what is happening, and that all information is getting relayed. It's a little bit like email, but not as personal I guess."

If she decides she can't cope with whatever her life would be and/or her body fails to respond—I will be honored to continue to be the go-between, to discuss everything—I can do it with three-way conversation on the cell phones, too. That way the information is more immediate and far more personal for everyone."

So my dear friend, I love you. I pray for everyone to win.—Lauren"

April 28 Email from Barb to me

"This has been a really sad and bad day for us, too. Ginny has continued to have seizures and has become totally unresponsive to anyone. Her eyes are closed and there is no response to stimulus. There will be more tests done on Monday, by the neurologists (who aren't there tomorrow) anyway, I think that's what John said. There were doctors there today, but they were unwilling to make any decisions—they need more data. They did say that the seizing wasn't a good sign. So what you're saying about Ginny's awareness of this is both amazing to me and also heartbreaking. We've decided to fly back there on Monday to say goodbye, if necessary. So tomorrow we'll be around, if you get any more communications."—Barb

April 29 5:15 a.m.

Ginny woke me up again, angry and agitated. I could practically feel her pace the floor, talking about life, about her coma. She was upset and unhappy at the situation. I attempted to counsel her but she wouldn't let herself be comforted.

"I'm going to die, aren't I?" she asked me.

"Yes," I said gently, "I believe you will. But dying will be easier than you think. The spirit realm is a pretty wonderful place. And you will see everyone you love again—in time."

"You think so?"

"Yes."

Ginny left abruptly without comment.

April 30 Dinnertime

Barb and her husband Ron had flown to Boston to be with John and Anna. Barb called me from the hospital in the evening. The news was grim.

"There's hardly any brain activity. Tomorrow at noon the doctors will discontinue life support, per Ginny's written request from her living will," Barb advised me.

May 1 5 a.m.

I was awakened by a furious spirit. "You're not my family. I don't want you talking to Barb or John. I want you to leave us alone. Don't pass on any more messages."

"Okay," I told Ginny gently. "I promise I won't do anything else." Without any further explanation, the spirit left abruptly.

I never heard from Ginny again. At noon the respirator was unplugged and Ginny's body died a few hours later. An autopsy was performed; then her body was cremated. Half of her ashes stayed in Boston, the rest went home for Barb's family to distribute. The autopsy showed severe heart problems—heart enlargement and multifocal scarred heart muscle. No one was aware of her heart problems. Because of that, Barb and her adult children are seeing cardiologists for follow up. Perhaps Ginny was acting as an angel, looking out for the family's health.

Postscripts

Newly-deceased spirits I have worked with have shown confusion, fear, and sometimes a desire to pass on a message to a loved one. Never have I seen an angry one. However, Ginny's body was living and her feisty spirit was attached to it. Ginny was officially "alive." She did not take an opportunity to go deep into the spirit realm for peace, although I encouraged her to do so.

For Barb, hers was an experience to know her sister was alive beyond physical existence, and would always be so. Barb had proof of their connection because of the synchronicity and timing of Ginny's remarks coupled with actual events going on in her hospital room—always within a moment of what was happening in Boston at her bedside.

The experience was a reminder to me that simply because a person is asleep, in surgery, or in a coma, it does not mean that person is "gone," but is actually present and aware. I felt honored that I was allowed to pass on the messages that I did, to embrace the wishes of Ginny's spirit and her family.

June 22, 2012 T
Telephone Conversation with Barb. I wanted to call Barb to make sure I had the dates and events correct before I finalized this article. She confirmed the following dates:

Ginny's cardiac arrest and lapse into coma—**April 25, 2012**
Ginny's body died—**May 1 , 2012**

Barb has never shared the information I gave her about Ginny with anyone except her husband Ron, but she plans to send John my article at an appropriate time.

John had an experience he believes was Ginny trying to communicate with him. He returned home to Washington from Boston around May 4th or 5th. He was lying in bed, trying to go to sleep. The bed began shaking and he felt a stroking feeling on his feet through the blankets. He got spooked, and went downstairs to his office. As he went in, a smoky sphere followed him, which circled the computer and then disappeared. The experience left him scared and shaky. Before she died, Ginny used to wake John up for work in the morning by shaking the bed.

Barb went to a cardiologist and brought Ginny's autopsy with her. According to the autopsy, Ginny had heart problems which led to her cardiac arrest: "cardiac hypertrophy in the setting of mild coronary artery disease associated with an arrhythmic event at the time the patient was found to be unresponsive." The autopsy mentioned brain damage to the front temporal lobes. The cardiologist was grateful as it was helpful in prescribing a proper medication for Barb, who has been having irregular heartbeats (arrhythmias) for a year or so. As the doctor looked over Ginny's records, he was sad. "If a cardiologist had seen her records or known what was going on, maybe Ginny could have been helped. Maybe her death might even have been prevented."

When I mentioned Huddie's participation the first day, and my conclusions, Barb was surprised. "How did you know Ginny had brain damage?" she asked me.

"I must have intuited it," I replied. There are many things I know that I can't explain."

As I discussed the general tenor of this article with Barb, I wanted to be sympathetic yet correct in judging Ginny's personality—including her taking charge, her abrupt comings and goings, and her angry attitude at the end.

Barb laughed and said, "Sounds just like Ginny." Barb continued: "Ginny's emotions also sound like that of a person who is trying to cope with all the grim ramifications of coma, serious illness, and ultimately death." Furthermore, Barb clarified: "Before the angry exchange with Ginny, you had offered to me, on the phone, to pass on messages from Ginny to us and vice versa—to be a go-between. Then Ginny reacted to this with the 'You're not family angry message.'"

Barb had a disquieting experience with Ginny's doctor when the doctor and family were gathered around a table to discuss discontinuing Ginny's life support while Ginny's body was still officially alive.

The doctor said, "The comforting thing is that Ginny went to sleep next to her beloved partner and never woke up."

Barb completely trusts my experiences of Ginny's presence. She knew what the doctor said might not be correct, but she didn't feel okay to mention her involvement with me and Ginny's spirit.

To doctors and families: When in the presence of a comatose person or one under general anesthesia, be respectful as though the person is standing in front of you, fully alive and able to communicate.

After writing this article and talking with Barb I have a renewed sense of commitment to inform others what happens in the spirit realm. We don't know what is going on with the spirit/personality of a comatose person. The same could be true of someone during surgery, experiencing dementia, mental retardation, autism, or any other condition in which the spirit is alive and well, but the physical body and mind cannot communicate properly.

Every person is alive, conscious, and able to communicate—albeit on a subtle level. A spirit is truly immortal—it doesn't die, but lives on in realms of time/space/dimensions we can only imagine. I'm proud to have participated with Ginny in her struggle for survival and the desire to communicate her wishes to her family. Bless you, Ginny, wherever you are and whatever you're doing. I will never forget you.

One of my gifts is clairaudience (psychic hearing)

My Life With Fairies and Devas

—⚬—

In January 2004, Paul and I moved to Whidbey Island, in the state of Washington, to start a permaculture and survival farm on two-and-a-half acres. Permaculture is organic farming plus growing food like nature does—including many different species growing together, which makes the whole more resilient and stronger than its parts. The farm had been pastureland for twenty-five years. We planted fruit and nut trees, twelve kinds of berries, currants, herbs, wild flowers, and a 3,000 square foot vegetable garden—from scratch.

The first week we were there I went out into the field and prayed out loud. I asked for help from the spirits of the land, soil, insects, birds, reptiles, animals, and plants to help guide me and teach me the way of nature. Then I asked that the whole area (including neighbors and a nearby gun club) be brought into one harmonious "family." I blithely thanked "everyone" and went back into the house. I had no idea what would emerge from my asking.

The next week I was sitting at our dining room window, looking out at our embryonic farm. I could see hundreds, maybe thousands of tiny bright lights flying into the field. Although I had never seen Fairies before, I knew instinctively, and from reading, the lights were Fairies. The Fairies celebrated that night with a huge party, then settled onto a large fir tree, making it their home. In the ensuing years, whenever I had a problem with the farm, I would go to the fir tree and "talk" to the Fairies psychically. They either advised me what actions to take or took care of the problem themselves. Both methods worked quite well.

Whenever we needed manure or compost, materials, or help, I asked. Whatever we needed showed up, sometimes within hours.

Truckloads of composting material showed up but, after six months, we noticed that the rodent population had exploded. We could see mice and voles running all over. I commented to Paul that maybe we should visit the nearest animal shelter and get some barn cats. The Fairies must have overheard us because the next day three feral cats showed up—a hefty tabby I named Mr. Kitty, his wife Diamond, and his son Slick. We fed them, got them fixed, and they stayed with us for eight years. The three of them quickly reduced the rodents to manageable numbers. Over time, whenever I noticed the mice and vole numbers climbing, I talked to Mr. Kitty and showed him mental images of catching the critters. Within a day our porch was littered with half-eaten rodent carcasses.

I asked the Fairies to bring in helpful snakes and created rockeries for the slithery reptiles to live in. Soon after I began to see snakes among the tall grass.

Many people who came to our farm (to buy eggs and produce, help out, or just visit) told us that our farm reminded them of Findhorn. I had read about that miraculous Scottish farm, visited there in 1996 for a day, and felt flattered at the association. I decided to call upon the Nature Spirits (Devas), as had the founders of Findhorn. The first thing I did was go into the field and call upon the main Deva. He showed up immediately, with a booming voice and an immense presence, the size of two football fields put together. This Deva was in charge of overseeing many acres all around us. When I prayed that first week I had apparently contacted this Deva, who subsequently invited the Fairies. I thanked him for all his work on our behalf. He seemed pleased.

Later that day I decided I would also talk to the Devas for each of the individual crops. I began with the tomato plants I had started from seed indoors. I spoke out loud and asked the tomato Deva what, if anything, the tomato plants required. The reply was amazing.

"Silly woman," the Deva replied, "you have been communicating with all of us for years!"

I responded with surprise. "How did I do that?"

"You talk to us with your feeling-voice," it told me.

I assumed the feeling-voice meant my intuition.

"You can talk if you want to or you can go back to your usual style."

From that moment on, I made sure to say hello to all the plants and Devas any time I went outside. I also practiced saying "Please may I pick some" whenever I wanted to harvest anything, and "Thank you" after I had done so.

I also practiced thanking the chicken Deva for the eggs our hens laid. Because of my close and daily interaction with our free-range chickens, visitors admired how healthy, friendly, and loving our hens were. I delighted everyone when I called the chickens to me—"Darlings!" The hens knew my voice (I discovered that most birds are sound oriented) and would come running to me. Our visitors told us that our eggs were the best organic, free-range they had ever tasted. Apparently I had also used my feeling-voice with the chicken Deva.

Our next-door neighbor obtained a steer to raise on her pasture. I went down to meet him (the steer) and brought him some greens. While he munched I noticed his left eye was red, swollen, full of pus, and leaking nasty-looking fluid. I asked the main Deva to help the cow. The next day I brought the steer some more greens and was amazed to find that his eye was completely healed. Our neighbor Shelley came over to greet me.

"We were going to call the vet but we found that the eye was healed.

Lauren, did you have anything to do with the cow's eye healing? I told my Dad I was sure you did something."

I giggled. "Yes, I asked the Deva to help the cow's eye yesterday. Let's thank the Deva right now." I closed my eyes and quickly thanked the Deva for his help. Awesome!

It worked with humans, too. At one point we had some difficulties with the neighboring gun club and I asked the Deva to help with the problems. Within a week all had been easily smoothed over without my even needing to talk to anyone from the gun club.

The last experiences we had on our farm were two-fold. We weren't able to keep up the farm anymore. I was ill and Paul was getting too old. I asked for help in selling the farm. Within one day, and without a realtor, we had sold the farm for our asking price to a family who had been looking for a farm for five years!

Shortly before we moved away Mr. Kitty got very sick, lost so much weight that his ribs stuck out, wheezed constantly, and could hardly walk. I thought he was dying. I asked the main Deva to help (I thought he would help Mr. Kitty die easily.) I didn't see the cat for a few days. Then Mr. Kitty showed up, looking much better. Within two weeks he was back to his healthy, plump self. Of course, I thanked the Deva for all his work.

Working with Fairies and Devas brought many miracles to our farm and helped me to appreciate the wonders of the unseen world of nature spirits. We live in an amazing universe!

Memoriam For Paul

—m—

I was forty-three. I had just left my current boyfriend after five grueling years, and was staying in a battered woman's shelter for a month. For three years I had attended Co-Dependents Anonymous, a Twelve-Step group. I continued to work my steps during my time in the shelter. I was very bad at picking men to be in relationships with—or else I was very good at picking awful men. I prayed to my higher power to pick out a good man and send him to me.

Soon after that I landed a secretarial job in the English Department at California State University, Fullerton. My Council of Elders, whom I had worked with for thirty-nine years, began sending me a telepathic message every day, "Be patient. Your beloved is coming." Every day for six months they sent the message, "Your beloved is coming." I didn't believe them, not after all the difficulties I'd had in my life.

At work I was told about Dr. Paul O. a professor of Comparative Literature. He lived in Amsterdam with his wife, traveled to California to teach one semester a year, then returned home. He would be arriving soon.

One day in late January I was seated at my desk typing when Dr. O. strolled in through the back door of the department. I looked up from my typewriter and our eyes met. He seemed very familiar. An instant friend. We smiled and introduced ourselves.

For the next several weeks our friendship grew. We talked every spare minute we could. I was very comfortable with him. Suddenly I realized that Paul was interested in me and I was falling in love with him. Big trouble! He was married and living in Amsterdam. "Oh, no." I stopped talking with him except on departmental business.

Out of the blue Paul invited me to dinner, to explain his situation to me.

I said yes. *Yes? Lauren, are you crazy? Well, it's just dinner,* I rationalized.

At dinner he told me he was lonely. He explained that before we met, he had often imagined a Dutch woman, blonde, blue-eyed, and slender. I'm half Dutch, blonde, blue-eyed, and was slender in those days. We began dating.

On our second date Paul came to my front door to pick me up to take me to dinner. When I opened the door, I was swept away with intense emotion stemming from a past life. I fell to my knees, put my arms around his legs, and sobbed. "I've missed you so much!" I exclaimed.

"But I just saw you yesterday," he replied—rational and unruffled as usual.

Later I told him about the past life I had experienced when I opened the door. We were brother and sister on a tiny island in Polynesia. Our parents were the local king and queen, also brother and sister. When we were old enough, Paul (my brother) and I would marry and become the next king and queen. Therefore, we were encouraged to be not only loving but lovers. Our wedding was being planned, but before we could marry, my brother contracted a fever and suddenly died. I could never marry anyone else because I was could only marry my brother and thus would remain alone the rest of my life. I never got over my sorrow at losing him—my sibling, my lover, my friend—and "I" died a few years later.

On my third date with Paul, I remembered the Elders' message. I impulsively asked him: "Are you my beloved?"

Without hesitation or asking what I meant, both uncharacteristic of him, he replied, "Yes."

When Paul returned to Amsterdam at the end of the semester, his wife told him she was moving to Munich. Paul immediately moved to California to be with me. That was twenty-four years ago. He was sixty-six. I was forty-three.

Paul was a brilliant man. He earned a Ph.D. in Comparative Literature and taught English, Literature, and Psychology for over fifty years. He went back to school, got an Masters in Psychology, and became a practicing psychologist. He wrote several books, *The New Scientist* and *Mirrors of Man*. With his best friend in the music department, they created a Choral Symphony entitled *The Wheel of Time*. In the 1960s he encouraged the University to tear out all the concrete and put in vegetable gardens, to teach students how to grow and sell food. He was a man ahead of his time.

He created a highly popular Interdisciplinary Center which merged traditional and non-traditional, even mystical, courses of study. He created a Counseling department to teach students to be counselors, and a new Religious Studies department, although he himself was not a religious man. Yet he had an abiding curiosity about consciousness. Paul was an eclectic, a renaissance thinker, someone who could talk for hours about a piece of literature, what period in which it was set, what the social milieu consisted of, the politics, the religion, philosophy, psychology, and other factors that molded the writer and the work. When Paul taught and lectured, he lit up from the inside.

He wasn't dogmatic, but preferred to continually gain knowledge and information and discuss concepts. He was consistently cheerful, loving, and kind, living in equanimity. His dear friend Michael on Whidbey Island called him the Buddha. Although we could sometimes drive each other crazy, I always knew I loved him and that he loved me.

Paul was a humanist and believed that when he died, his body would just die, be gone, literally fall to dust. There was no god, no universe, no higher power that he believed in. He had faith in and practiced love and being a good person. He unconditionally believed my extensive spiritual experiences while having none of his own.

For two years I watched Paul going steadily downhill physically. In 2012 he had a heart attack and two stents were inserted. He was put on strong medications which affected him dramatically. His ankle tendons gave out and it was hard for him to walk. His back became crooked and he lost several inches of height.

Then he was diagnosed with colon cancer. Paul didn't want to go through chemo or radiation. The surgeon thought Paul would recover splendidly with surgery and we consented.

I'm a healer and attempted two spiritual healings on Paul, but the cancer didn't go away. I asked Paul if he'd let me put my hands on him and he agreed. He sat down on a kitchen chair. I stood behind him and put my hands on his head. Tremendous spiritual energy came coursing through me and into Paul. For thirty minutes I could feel the transmitted power, but didn't know what Paul was experiencing.

When it was done, he related that he had floated out of his body and into a reality that was filled with love and peace. All the people he had known in his life paraded in front of him. Each one was connected to him with love. He was blissed out. He told me that experience changed his life forever. He excitedly telephoned everyone he knew to tell of his miraculous occurrence.

But...I knew he was preparing to die.

I cried, inconsolable, for days.

On the following Tuesday, Paul went into the hospital and had surgery. I could tell when he arrived in his hospital room after recovery that things were bad. His kidneys were failing. The next morning he was transferred to ICU. He kept telling everyone he was going home on Saturday.

By early Saturday morning his children and grandchildren had flown in to be with him, although at the end he was unconscious under morphine.

As I stood at Paul's side I touched his face gently. "Honey, if you want to leave, you can. We're all here now. We all love you. We will always love you. Remember your miraculous experience. There's nothing to be afraid of. So, if you want to go, you can go now."

Within five minutes he left his body. The spark that was Paul vanished. I held his hand as it turned cold, while his family and I sat in the ICU room with him. Keeping him company for the next hour, waiting for the mortician to arrive.

For three days Paul's spirit stayed with me, talking to me, comforting me.

Then a group of beings came to him. "It's time to go," they advised and I felt him start to drift away. A plug of energetic connection was painfully yanked from my heart, while Paul returned to the spirit realm.

A week later Paul's essence returned momentarily, now clothed in his magnificent spirit body. He sparkled with health, vitality, and a youthful, handsome countenance. He grinned in delight. "I need to go show the girls," he announced, and poof, was gone.

A few days later Paul showed up yet again, this time in the area where my Elders resided. I was confused and a question passed through my mind.

"I've joined the Elders," he explained.

I knew I could communicate with him through that group upon occasion. Then, like an idle thought, he disappeared.

Our relationship wasn't perfect. We weren't perfect people. We loved. We argued. We traveled. We disagreed, fought, and cried. We adored movies and going out to eat. We had different likes and dislikes, dissimilar styles of expressing ourselves. He was a philosopher, and like Socrates, (or was it Plato?) he questioned everything and everyone. I'm a pragmatist and trust my experiences. We talked incessantly. We gardened. We farmed for seven years. We raised chickens. We made love. We were quiet. We helped his kids and my kids, his grandchildren and my grandchildren through rough spots. We moved a lot. I was sick a lot. We bought and sold houses.

He was everything. My home. My peaceful repose. My safety net. My love.

We were best friends, lovers, partners, beloved companions, inseparable even in the hardest times. He was my darling. I miss him.